NOT THE FUHRER'S SON

The True Story of a Young Boy's
Survival in Nazi Germany

Werner J. Stamm M.D.

Velvet Fig, Inc.

CALIFORNIA

Copyright © 2022 by Werner J Stamm MD

All rights reserved. No part of this publication may be reproduced, distributed or transmitted in any form or by any means, including photocopying, recording, or other electronic or mechanical methods, without the prior written permission of the author, except in the case of brief quotations embodied in critical reviews and certain other noncommercial uses permitted by copyright law. For permission requests, write to the author.

Werner J Stamm MD
stammrichmas@gmail.com

Published by Velvet Fig, Inc.
Los Gatos, California

Not the Fuhrer's Son/ Werner J Stamm MD. -- 1st ed.
ISBN 979-8-9850942-3-7

Dedication

*This book has been inspired by and is dedicated
to my parents, Mrs. Anna Stamm and Mr. Max Stamm.*

*My mother, especially, showed unbelievable courage
and determination throughout the war
as well as during the postwar period,
which at times seemed more difficult
than the war years.*

*For all I have accomplished in my life,
she has been the main source
of my strength and determination.*

Contents

1 SUMMER CAMP 3
2 HOME AGAIN 7
3 AT WAR 9
4 LIFE AT HOME 13
5 WEDDING ANNIVERSARY, HIJACKED 15
6 OPA'S DEMISE 17
7 PLANNING FOR THE FUTURE 19
8 CHANGING FORTUNES 21
9 PARTY TIME 29
10 CLOSE CALL 31
11 OBERHOF 35
12 BLINDED 41
13 SIMONE 43
14 GARDELEGEN 47
15 FINSTERBERGEN 49
16 THE ESCAPE 53
17 MESCHEDE 59
18 HOME AGAIN 63
19 APRIL 1945, SOLDIER FOR A DAY 69
20 HORSE TRADING 71
21 THE AMERICANS ARE HERE 73
22 THE VACUUM 75
23 HAMSTERN 79
24 TO KILL THE GOOSE 83
25 AMERICAN OCCUPATION 87
26 HENRY THE ROOSTER 89
27 LOTTI 93
28 THE HONEST THIEF 95

29 BACK TO SCHOOL	97
30 NEW STUDENTS	101
31 THE GENIUS	103
32 VACATION IN BAVARIA	107
33 MAKE ME A BUBERL!	111
34 JOINING THE BAND	115
35 PARIS, PARIS!	119
36 HEADING SOUTH	123
37 THE WATZMANN EXPERIENCE	125
38 HAPPY BIRTHDAY!	127
39 HOMEBOUND DISASTER	129
40 CALL FROM THE EMBASSY	133
41 GHOST IN THE CLOSET	135
42 ACCEPTED FOR IMMIGRATION	137
43 FINAL EXAMINATION	139
44 GETTING READY FOR DEPARTURE	141
45 GOODBYE, SOLINGEN	143
46 HAMBURG	145
47 GOODBYE, GOODBYE!	147
48 UNDERWAY	149
49 STORMY WEATHER	151
50 NEW YORK, NEW YORK	153
51 MISS ROTHCHILD	155
52 GOING WEST	159
53 CHICAGO	161
54 VISIT TO DENVER	165
55 CALIFORNIA, I HAVE ARRIVED!	167
56 MY MOTHER'S STORIES	169
ACKNOWLEDGMENTS	173

FOREWORD

The events described in this book are true and describe my and my family's life in Germany from my early childhood, growing up in Solingen, Germany, up to my arrival in San Francisco, USA, as a young immigrant at age twenty, in 1952.

They include the times shortly before World War II, the almost seven years of World War II, and the postwar years from 1945 to 1952.

No events and no names have been changed.

CHAPTER ONE

SUMMER CAMP

It was July 1939. I sat between my parents in the back of Uncle Fritz's car. I was going home, finally, after four agonizing weeks.

My parents had meant well. It was true. I was an undernourished-looking, skinny kid. I just did not like to eat. My mother was a good cook. My father was accustomed to good home-cooked meals. Mother had one complaint about Father. "You never tell me that the food I cook tastes good!"

"If it didn't, I would tell you," he replied. That was the best compliment he could make.

Mother was very organized. She had a meal schedule which made things easy for her. Lunch was the main meal of the day, served at 12:30 PM when Father came upstairs from his knife factory in the back of the house. Meals were named by the dominant vegetable. There was always a small portion of some type of meat, but that was variable. On Mondays, it was beans. On Tuesdays, red cabbage. On Thursdays, it was always sauerkraut

Saturdays were special: pork chops with boiled potatoes, gravy, and a special vegetable, such as asparagus. Father loved pork chops. I can still see him chewing with delight, fat droplets running down his chin.

Sundays the kitchen was closed. We went out to dinner. It was always the same restaurant one block away. There was a small band playing live music. Mother had a plate of mussels, and Father and I had pork chops.

Mother and I often battled it out over eating. Anything I did not like, like a small piece of onion or vegetable, or a sliver of fat attached to meat, I transferred to the rim of the plate, often forming a large circle. Mother always watched me with mounting anger. I often stopped eating. When she urged me to continue, I usually said "The food is cold." She then grabbed my plate and heated up the food. (This was not easy since there was no such thing as a microwave oven). I then again sat there looking at the hot food, still not eating. And it got cold again.

It was a constant battle. Mother had heard about a summer recreation program for boys in Solingen Ohligs, a suburb of Solingen. She thought I would eat better and gain some weight there, being with other boys.

It was the summer of 1939. I was enrolled in a six-week program, which however had started two weeks before I got there.

Uncle Fritz drove my parents and me. We got there in the early afternoon.

The center consisted of a large one-story building on flat land with a scattering of tall pine trees. The compound was enclosed by a 6-foot cyclone fence.

We rang the bell at the entrance gate. After a minute or so a woman emerged from the building and came to the gate. My parents explained who I was. She opened the gate and motioned me in.

"How old are you?" she asked.

"Seven," I said, "almost eight".

I said goodbye to my parents and then followed the woman to the building, carrying my suitcase.

We entered a long hallway. She opened a side door and waved me in. "Wait here," she said. "The boys are taking their afternoon nap."

She closed the door behind me. I looked around. I was in a large sparsely furnished room with some tables and chairs. From the windows I saw scattered pine trees.

I sat down and waited. The place was dead quiet. After a while, I walked around a little, looking out the windows. Nobody out there.

Time went by slowly. I felt pressure building in my bladder. I had to go to the bathroom. I walked over to the door. It was locked. I knocked. No response. I knocked again, louder. Nothing. I called out, hoping somebody would hear me. I listened. Nothing.

The pressure in my bladder increased by the minute. I had to go, really go!

I finally heard voices in the hallway. Kids were coming. Someone unlocked my door. A woman with a commanding presence said to me, "Stand in line with those boys over there!"

I said, "I have to go to the bathroom." She paid no attention to me. She pushed me forward into line. I stepped out of line and told her again, but she shoved me back.

"You stand here!" she said.

I could not hold it any longer. I was wearing shorts. I watched the warm urine running down my right leg, into my shoe, and on the floor. I was mortified. I just stood there. The kids around me pointed and laughed. I felt like I wanted to sink into the ground.

That was my introduction to the camp.

I never felt comfortable there. I never made any friends. We slept in a big dorm. One of the kids was a bedwetter. When we got up in the morning, several boys ran over to his bed to check if his mattress was wet. They then howled and laughed and pointed fingers at the kid. He would just stand there, crying. I never talked with him, but I felt very sorry for him.

The days went by very slowly. The food was ok, except for one dish, which made me sick just looking at it. It was a Jello-like red desert with little round black specks like frog eggs. It would wiggle back and forth when I moved the bowl. It was served several times during those four weeks, and I was made to eat it, like it or not. I always gagged on it, trying to swallow. I had to force it down.

There was a two-hour rest period after lunch. We had to lie on cots on a large patio outside the building.

An attendant walked around watching us. There was no talking. Not once could I sleep. I would close my eyes when the attendant was close. One day, while looking around on the grounds, I found a small piece of metal that had been a piece of a can opener. It saved me from extreme boredom after that. I broke pieces of bark from pine trees, and during the two-hour rest period, I carved little boats and other things quietly and unnoticed. I had to clean up my workplace of course before leaving.

Slowly the days went by. A big event was planned for the last day at the camp. A train ride across the highest railroad bridge in Europe, the Mungsten Bridge, 108 meters high, connecting Solingen to our neighbor city of Remscheid.

We were all looking forward to it. A bus took us to the train station. The weather was beautiful. We had our noses pressed to the windows as the train entered the bridge. We were so high looking down into the valley with the Wupper River below us, we had the feeling of flying.

We got back to camp in the early evening. It had been a wonderful day.

Then dinner was served. It was a wonderful brown gravy with sauteed hamburger meat over boiled potatoes, with a vegetable, my favorite.

But then came dessert. My most hated desert with the frog eggs. I sat there staring at it. I was not going to eat that. Then I felt this presence behind me. That woman was watching me. "Eat your desert!" I sat there, not moving. "Eat your desert," came the threatening command again. I put a spoonful into my mouth and gagged. I could not swallow it. She did not leave my side, leaning over me.

I jumped up, pushed my chair and her aside and raced to the bathroom. Then I vomited. I lost my entire dinner.

That was the end of my four-week recreational summer camp. I had lost three pounds, I found out later.

CHAPTER TWO

HOME AGAIN

We were on our way home from the camp in August 1939. Uncle Fritz and my parents had come to pick me up. I was listening to my uncle and father talk. The government was reporting that ethnic Germans living in Poland were being harassed by the Polish people and the Polish government. The German government felt strongly that it had to come to the aid of the German people being oppressed in Poland.

Uncle Fritz worried that after what had happened during the last two years, war was a likelihood. Just recently, Germany had annexed the independent country of Austria, to make it part of the German Reich (German Empire). Father mentioned that Hitler was actually born in Linz in Austria. But since his rise to power in Germany, he had forced his family to change their last name, so that nobody could easily look into his background.

Then, more recently, Hitler had annexed part of Czechoslovakia under the pretense that ethnic Germans living there wanted to belong to Germany.

I was so happy to be home again, and I ate Mother's cooking without complaints.

August 26 was my birthday. I was eight. I had a little birthday party at our house with my neighborhood friends, Rolf and Ruth Schmidt, who lived two houses up, and Klaus, my downstairs neighbor. One funny thing happened the day before. We were all playing outside. Across from Rolf's house on the other side of the street was a vegetable garden behind a wire fence. We were digging in the dirt by the fence, when I came across a rusty metal pipe sticking out of the ground. The top was filled with dirt. As I started digging out some of the dirt, I noticed something shiny coming up. There were coins inside the pipe. I dug them out one at a time and ended up with a handful of money, totaling about 15 Deutsche Reich Marks, a whole treasure.

I showed my find to my friends and then ran home to show Mother.

She washed and dried the coins. They were real money!

Word got around in a hurry. The following day Klaus' mother from downstairs came up and knocked on our door. She told Mother she had heard about my find in the metal pipe. She stated that the money was actually hers. Her husband had a way of hiding money from her, and she was certain that he had stuffed it into the pipe. He used it for beer money, she stated.

Mother did not buy the story. The money was mine.

CHAPTER THREE

AT WAR

It was September 1939. The news came over the radio. German troops had invaded Western Poland and were making rapid progress against the retreating Polish army, liberating large numbers of ethnic Germans. The German Army was advancing against only mild Polish resistance. The newsreels in the movie theaters showed German tanks rolling past destroyed horse carriages of the Polish Army, and many dead Polish Army horses from the Polish Cavalry sent out to fight the German tanks. German Air Force planes were bombing Warsaw, the Capital of Poland.

The war was over in three weeks. It was named the Blitzkrieg (Lightning War).

But there was one problem, Father explained to me. A few years earlier a worried Polish government had signed a Mutual Defense Pact with England. A few days after the invasion of Poland, England and France declared WAR on Germany.

Both of my parents had grown up in and survived World War I as teenagers, when Germany was also fighting France and Britain in the West, as well as the Russians in the East.

It seemed like a replay of World War I.

Not long after, we heard that a British expeditionary force of forty thousand soldiers had landed in Dunkirk in northern France to assist the French Army.

The French were also reinforcing the Maginot Line from World War I, a massive defensive installation facing the equivalent German Siegfried Line, waiting for the attack from Germany.

The war with Poland in the East had ended, but now Germany was at war with France and England in the West.

Almost daily the German radio interrupted its regular program with announcements of victories in the West, always preceded by powerful martial music.

The German strategy this time was to not launch a frontal attack against France across the Maginot Line. Instead, the German army attacked France from the North, sweeping through totally unprepared Holland and Belgium. The British force in Dunkirk was routed and driven back into the sea.

France surrendered and German troops marched into Paris triumphantly without a shot having been fired there. Hitler triumphantly had the French Command sign the surrender papers in the same railroad car as the German command had to do in 1918, in the Forest of Compiegne in France.

The war seemed to be almost over. German troops had occupied Holland and Belgium as well as Denmark on the northern border. After that, Norway surrendered. Sweden declared neutrality. Italy, under Generalissimo Mussolini, became a German ally. The alliance acquired a formal name: The AXIS.

Spain declared its neutrality. German troops moved into Greece and landed paratroops on the island of Crete in the Mediterranean.

An expeditionary force was sent into Northern Africa under the Command of Field Marshal Erwin Rommel, to control the Suez Canal, which at that time was under British administration.

Only one problem remained. England was at war with Germany but being an island, it was protected from invasion by the English Channel and the Atlantic Ocean.

England was being supplied with armaments, food and other materials by ship from the United States.

We heard over the radio that the German Luftwaffe had begun the bombing of British military installations, especially air bases, and of industrial installations, in preparation for an Invasion of England. London was also being bombed, the London Blitz.

A large German U-Boat fleet was active in the Atlantic attacking and sinking ships supplying England. Often, two or three announcements of Victories at Sea came over the radio in one day.

CHAPTER FOUR

LIFE AT HOME

Our lives were not affected much for a long time. I was in Grammar School. My school was located up the street, about 1 block away from our house. Frau Hosse had been my teacher for the first two years. She was a very kind and gentle woman whom I really liked. I worked hard for her, and I had earned a seat in the back of the classroom. Poor students were seated in the front, right under the teacher's nose.

For the third and fourth grade we had a male teacher whom we did not like. He was nervous and often flew into fits of anger. He sometimes apologized afterward and explained that as a soldier in World War I a bullet had grazed the side of his head, which still affected him.

By midafternoon, with homework done, the kids in my neighborhood usually got together to play.

Our favorite activity was to run down our street past Mr. Weck's chicken ranch and into the Bearenloch, a wide heavily wooded canyon with a small brook flowing through it. We played there, building small forts out of tall fern, damming up the brook here and there, and fighting with the kids living on the other side of the canyon. Our favorite thing was to nail an empty cigar box to the tip of a fir tree. We would load the box with rocks, bend the tree way back and then catapult the rocks toward the enemy. We never hit anything or anybody but had great fun doing it.

One time the kids from the other side attacked us and drove us back up our hill. Two of the kids grabbed me, while my friends were running away.

I was tied to a tree and just left there. I yelled and squirmed, trying to free myself. Nobody heard me. Ants started to crawl up my legs. I could not fight them off, with my arms tied behind me.

I kept yelling, and after what seemed to be forever, two adults came and freed me. My so-called friends never came back to look for me.

One of my classmates was the son of a farmer. One day he invited me over to the farm. They were going to slaughter a pig. He thought I might enjoy watching it.

When I got there a large pig had been roped around the neck and the rope fastened to a tree in the yard. The pig was snorting, grunting and obviously very anxious.

My friend's father stepped forward holding a long knife. He loosened the rope from the tree. A second man came holding an empty bowl. The man with the knife bent down and slit the pig's throat. I stood there horrified. Blood was pouring from the animal's neck. The pig squealed and tore itself loose from the rope. It raced across the orchard, back and forth, blood squirting from its throat, until it finally collapsed and lay there, its legs and body still jerking.

The animal was then dragged into the barn and lifted into a tub filled with hot water. The man with the empty bowl cursed that he was unable to collect the fresh blood for making blood sausage.

My classmate came running with a kitchen knife which he plunged repeatedly into the pig, laughing and having a great time, while the pig's body was being shaved.

I was thoroughly disgusted and angry. I walked home.

CHAPTER FIVE

WEDDING ANNIVERSARY, HIJACKED

It was the summer of 1943. My father's parents, my grandparents Emma and Otto (Opa) Stamm, were looking forward to celebrating their 50th wedding anniversary. All members of the family, as well as neighbors and friends, had been invited to the party which was to be held in the hall of a neighborhood restaurant. It was to start midafternoon with coffee and cake, followed by dinner.

My parents and I, as well as a few other family members, walked over to the restaurant a few hours early to see that everything was set up properly.

To our surprise several men in brown Nazi uniforms were there, decorating the hall. We asked them what they were doing. We were told that the Wedding Couple was being honored by the NSDAP, the official name of the Nazi Party. My grandparents were not members of the Party, nor was the rest of the family, except for one uncle.

We did not dare object and just watched.

The Wedding Couple was to be seated at the head and center of a wide and long T-shaped table. Behind the table the wall had been draped with a large Swastika Nazi Flag.

The tables were being decorated with small vases containing fresh flowers and Nazi flags.

There was nothing for us to do. We did not dare ask any critical questions or make any adverse comments. My grandparents, arriving in the afternoon, were wide-eyed and speechless. This was not the party we all had planned.

After everyone, including guests, was seated, a smartly uniformed Brown Shirt got up, raised his outstretched right arm and shouted "Heil Hitler." He walked over to my grandmother and placed a golden paper crown on her head. He then launched into a speech, praising my grandparents as representing a typical proud German couple; industrious, having raised eight children, in the spirit of the Third Reich, loyal to the Fuhrer.

He then started into a Nazi Party song, which everybody was obliged to join in. After that the Brownshirts left, the atmosphere became relaxed, and coffee and cake were served.

We never found out who had notified the Nazis of the wedding anniversary party. But the following day a photograph of my grandparents was in the local newspaper, my grandmother wearing her golden paper crown, a big Nazi flag behind her.

CHAPTER SIX

OPA'S DEMISE

It was about six months later. There was a knock on our door very early in the morning. Mother answered. My grandmother was standing there in her long nightgown.

"Opa is dead!" she said.

Mother got dressed quickly and followed my grandmother to her house, which was located next to ours. Mother told us the story later. Grandfather was lying in their bed, on his back. The skin of his face was white. His eyes were half closed, his mouth wide open. He was obviously dead. Grandmother stated that she had slept in the same bed all night. When she awoke in the morning, Opa was not moving. He had died during the night.

Mother knew what to do.

For reasons I never understood, she was fascinated with death and was not afraid of a dead human body. She often took a detour through the local cemetery on her way to shopping in the city, hoping she would see a skeleton being excavated. If someone died, neighbors would call her to wash the body.

Opa was wearing a long nightgown. Mother removed it with some difficulty. She then got a bowl of warm soapy water with which she washed the entire body. She then dressed the body in a fresh clean nightgown. But she had one problem. Opa's mouth was wide open. It had to be closed before viewing by the family and neighbors later.

She got a towel, slung it under his chin, knotted it on top of his head and pulled hard until his mouth was closed. It worked fine for a while. But then she noticed the jaw slowly dropping. She repeated the maneuver several times, but without lasting success.

The Funeral Home had been called in the meantime. When the Funeral Director arrived, Mother told him about her dilemma. "No problem," he said. He pulled a match box from his pocket and propped it under Opa's chin, effectively closing his mouth. He told Mother not to remove it until the body was stiff. It worked. Mother was delighted. The mouth stayed closed.

After two days, when all family members and friends had said goodbye to Opa, the body was taken to the Funeral Home.

CHAPTER SEVEN

PLANNING FOR THE FUTURE

Fall came and I heard my parents discussing my future. In Germany at that time, the vast majority of children finished 8 years of elementary school, at age 14. If they choose to work in a trade, they would then go to trade school for 2 years. At age 16, they would take 2 years of practical training as an apprentice in that trade, and then enter a journeyman program. This would also include evening classes in a structured vocational program. After passing a final test at 20, they would get a Meister (Master) degree which would entitle them to open their own business, and to also teach their trade.

If one wanted a higher education in the field of business, politics, law or medicine, one would leave elementary school at the age of 10 (after fourth grade), and then enter High School. The High School curriculum would be 8 years, ending with a High School diploma at age 18.

My father felt that I should work in his trade, which was the knife industry. All his male family members were knife makers. "What's good enough for me is good enough for Werner," he said.

My father had only six years of grammar school education. At age twelve he had to drop out of school to work in his father's knife factory, since his older brothers had all been drafted into the army in World War I.

Mother said, "No! Making knives is a dirty business where people die at an early age." It was true. Most workers developed "stone lung" (Silicosis), after inhaling silicone from grind stones, wood and metal dust for most of their working lives, ending up with severe emphysema and death from pulmonary insufficiency.

"Werner is going to High School. He is going to be a lawyer or a doctor."

There was no doctor or lawyer in my entire family. And nobody had gone beyond a Grammar School education.

Mother won. I was enrolled in one of the two boys' High Schools in Solingen, the Humboldt School, after passing an entrance examination. There was a monthly fee of 20 Deutsche Marks, which Mother said we could afford.

I found out that I was the only student in my grammar school class of 40 to go to High School that year.

CHAPTER EIGHT

CHANGING FORTUNES

It was 1941. Two years had already gone by since the war started, and we had not really been touched by it yet. But things were about to change.

Uncle Willi, my mother's younger brother, had been drafted into the army. He was a tool and die maker by trade, but his passion was music. He played several wind instruments as a member of a local dance band on weekends. The army assigned him to a military band in occupied Holland.

Uncle Fritz was drafted into the Army and was stationed in Paris, France. He was having a good time and often sent us packages with hard-to-get food including sausages and real coffee.

Uncle Kurt, my father's younger brother, was drafted into the Army and was assigned to a motorcycle unit. He was given a new BMW bike which he loved.

Cousin Guenter was about six years older than I. He had just graduated from High School as Valedictorian of his class. He had a photographic memory. He told me once that he could study best at home by walking back and forth in their living room, book in hand, classical music playing in the background. Upon graduation from High School the entire class was told it would be an honor for all students to volunteer for the Armed Forces. Guenter joined the Army, together with all his classmates.

But slowly, things began to change.

There were nightly bombing raids on German cities by large formations of enemy bombers. More and more frequently, air raid sirens would get us out of bed in the middle of the night. We would throw on some clothes, grab our suitcases sitting in the hallway, packed with essential things, and hurry downstairs into the basement. There we would sit with the other tenants in our house, waiting for the "All Clear" siren. Most often nothing would happen, and we would climb back into bed after an hour or so.

After a while we got so used to being roused from sleep, that we tended to stay upstairs in our apartment after getting dressed, rather than heading for the basement. We would sit by the radio and listen to what was happening. Every household had a map of Europe with coordinates. Our map was fastened to the wall next to the radio. The announcer would describe something like "Heavy Enemy Formations entering from Holland, coordinates XX, heading towards coordinates XX." We could follow the progress of the enemy planes that way. If it seemed that they were not coming close to our area, we would go back to bed. If the planes got close to our area, we still would wait upstairs.

Not infrequently we could hear enemy planes approaching. Anti-aircraft searchlights, stationed in a field behind and not far from our house, would light up and crisscross the sky with white light fingers. When they caught a plane, usually cruising along up high, they would hold the plane in their beam for a while, then hand it over to the next search light battery. Anti-aircraft batteries would then go into action, and we could see the explosions around the plane. It became very exciting. We would then listen to where the shrapnel fragments were landing with a swishing sound, so that we could find and pick them up in the morning. I collected quite a few of them, some vicious looking ones with jagged edges, six to eight inches long. All the kids in the neighborhood had their own collections.

The government then started to give instructions in home defense. The windows of all buildings had to be blackened out at dark, so that enemy planes could see no lights on the ground for orientation. All streetlights were turned off. Automobile headlights were reduced to narrow horizontal slits. People walking outside at dark were wearing quarter sized green, fluorescent buttons on their coats or jackets so that they would not collide with others on the sidewalk or on the street.

All adults in our neighborhood had to go to our grammar school yard for instructions as to how to put out fires from magnesium and phosphorus bombs. Magnesium bombs were hexacanth foot long sticks of aluminum, about two inches in diameter. Water or sand would extinguish those.

Phosphorus bombs were foot long metal canisters filled with jellied phosphorus. Only sand or dirt would extinguish them by depriving the phosphorus of oxygen.

Each house was furnished with large buckets of water and hand pumps, as well as sandbags, to be placed on the landing of each floor, as well as in the attic.

We had heard about the death of hundreds of civilians in bombing raids trapped in their home basement shelters. As a result, each house owner was now required to dig an open-air trench for shelter in the back of their property.

Father and I dug such a trench in our backyard. About three feet wide and five to six feet deep, with a zigzag pattern, about fifteen feet long. But it was not useful. After a rain, it was partially filled with water and mud. The chickens liked to go down there and leave their business. We had to clean up the trench all the time. We only used it once during an air raid.

Slowly the general mood began to change. There were less victory pronouncements over the radio. Food rationing was introduced. Each person received a card with coupons for 30 days of food. Excepted from rationing were vegetables, which most people grew in their own gardens. On the other hand, food listed on the cards was not always available.

One day Mother said, "Werner, run down to the North Sea fish market and get some herring for us. I heard that a shipment just arrived."

She gave me our ration cards and I darted off. The market was downtown. As I got closer, I saw a long line of people standing on the sidewalk leading to the store. I joined the line. It must have been almost two hours before I got within 30 feet of the store. Then a person in an apron stepped out. "I am sorry, but we are all sold out. No more fish!"

Cooking fat or cooking oil and butter were difficult to find. Mother had a brilliant idea. Father was able to buy for the factory an industrial type of fat used for polishing knife handles. It was from the neck of cattle and had been treated with some chemical which made it unfit for human consumption. Mother experimented with the fat. She loaded up a large frying pan with it, added copious amounts of sliced onions, water, and then boiled the mixture on the kitchen stove.

The air turned blue, the smell was atrocious, but the end result was great. It did not kill us. We had cooking fat again.

There were air raids during the day now. We were told that the United States had entered the war on the side of Britain and France. It was 1941. Formations of US planes came to attack during the day, the British planes attacked during the night.

Not infrequently, while on the way to High School on the streetcar, the air raid sirens sounded, and we had to get off. We usually made it to a large air raid shelter in a natural cave underneath the Catholic Church in Wald, a suburb of Solingen. We often sat there, waiting for one or two hours before the ALL-CLEAR siren sounded. Sometimes school was out however, before we got to class.

One day Uncle Kurt, my father's younger brother, called. He had been notified that his only son, Klaus, together with Klaus' mother, had been killed in an air raid on the city of Koblenz, an ancient picturesque city on the Rhine River.

Uncle Willy, my father's older brother, was notified that his Valedictorian son Guenter was killed on the Russian front. He was shot through the head by a sniper bullet.

My younger cousin Heinz, son of my father's sister Ella, about 10 years old, was dead. He had been sent to a farm to be safe from the bombing raids. One day he was chasing a cat inside a barn. The cat dove underneath a hay turning machine. Heinz followed, driving two metal spikes into his forehead. His mother went out of her mind. She gave a party for her dead son at her house. I vividly remember her pulling the dentures out of her mouth, waving them at us, and crying hysterically.

My favorite grandmother, my mother's mother, lived upstairs in a three-story house on a hillside overlooking the entire area. I often visited her, staying overnight on weekends to keep her company.

One afternoon, as I was approaching her house on my bicycle, I heard airplanes. I looked up and saw two single-engine planes moving up very fast. I was in an open field. I got off my bike and threw myself to the ground. The planes flew over at low altitude. Then I saw what looked like bombs dropping from the planes, followed by a loud "BOOM, BOOM" of explosions and smoke. I waited a while, but nothing more happened. The planes did not return. Curious as to where the bombs had landed, I jumped on my bike and raced in the direction of the smoke.

After about 20 minutes I got there. Hiller's Chocolate and Peppermint factory had been hit. The large building was smoking, with small fires here and there. Bricks, together with other larger debris, were littering the street. Chunks of raw chocolate were lying everywhere in the debris. People had already arrived and were picking up chocolate.

I leaned my bike against a tree and started collecting chunks of raw chocolate. I had an arm full when I heard plane engines approaching. I stepped behind a big chestnut tree and waited. Two planes came over, perhaps the ones which had dropped the bombs. They made a leisurely turn and then disappeared. I got home with my chocolate without a problem.

People were talking. The war was not going well. One had to be careful as to whom you talked to. One could not say anything against Hitler, or there would be consequences.

My mother's twin brother Arthur had in the past been a member of the outlawed Communist Party. He would spout off sometimes against Hitler when he was in a pub, with too much to drink. Twice he was arrested and sent to jail. Once he was sentenced to hard labor. He was shipped to a swampy marsh somewhere together with other inmates. The prisoners had to dig trenches to drain the swamp manually, often standing up to their hips in water. He later developed chronic kidney disease.

Uncle Otto was one of my father's older brothers, a jovial man who worked in a local steel factory. He smoked cigars, which his wife Erna despised and forbade. But Uncle got away with it by hiding his cigars under his hat which he wore constantly, including in the house.

Tradition was that every Sunday morning all the adult children in my father's family came to my grandparents' house, where they drank coffee, had a shot of Schnapps or two, and talked. And, of course, the war was the main topic. And Hitler's name came up. The comments about Hitler and the war became more and more negative.

Uncle Otto was the only Nazi Party member in the family. At one point he became very upset when Hitler was criticized. He stated that from now on, if any of his brothers said anything negative about Hitler, he would report it to the Gestapo, brother or not. After that, conversation about the war and the Nazi Party ended.

Uncle Otto had one son from a previous marriage, Herbert. Herbert was about sixteen and worked in the same factory as his dad. The factory was broken into one night, and some tools were stolen. Herbert went to the management a few days later and confessed to being the person who had committed the burglary.

The police interviewed Herbert about the details of the burglary. They concluded that he did not know anything about the event and that his story was a fabrication.

After that, Uncle Otto and the people who worked with Herbert became more and more aware of his mental instability. Herbert was admitted to a mental institution eventually, located in a remote location in the Westerwald, an area about an hour's bus ride from Solingen.

One weekend, my parents and I accompanied Uncle Otto on a visit to Herbert. We took some food along for him. I was horrified to watch him attack the food like a starved animal. I never saw Herbert again.

One day Uncle Otto traveled to visit his son. When he arrived at the hospital, he was told that Herbert had passed away. Uncle was extremely upset and inquired about the details. Herbert had died several weeks prior, and his body had been buried in an unmarked location. Uncle Otto knew that the Nazis didn't want to support or care for people who contributed nothing or were a burden to society. The Nazis had killed his son. Uncle Otto changed his attitude about Hitler and the Nazi party.

I was later given some of Herbert's clothes and his bicycle.

CHAPTER NINE

PARTY TIME

The air raids on our area slowly became more frequent and everybody was becoming more pessimistic about the course of the war and about survival.

Slogans began to appear on the walls of buildings.

Sieg Heil , Wheels Have to Roll for Victory.

Careful, the Enemy Is Listening!

Kohlenklau, Save Energy, with a picture of an ugly one-eyed monster stealing coal.

In order to cope with increasing anxiety and depression, people decided to live it up with parties. Alcohol was available. We had parties every Saturday night, rotating between friends in the neighborhood. I still have a picture of my father standing with a glass of beer in his hand, with a kids' oval toy railroad track around his neck.

One evening, at a party in our apartment, Mr. Buechel, a butcher who lived downstairs, got very agitated and started hitting the wooden armrest of the chair he was sitting in, breaking it. We escorted him down to his place.

And then there was Fritz Rauh, a neighbor from down the street, a knife maker like my father. He had been drinking heavily and was getting sick. He got up and left our apartment to go down half a flight of stairs to the toilet.

Our six-family apartment house had a total of three toilets, each located off the staircase on a landing halfway between floors. Each consisted of a 4 by 4-foot lockable closet-like space with a toilet. The toilet consisted of a large wooden box shaped structure with a central open seat. An enameled large funnel shaped tube was attached underneath, connecting below floor level to a larger pipe. This then led into the large underground septic tank behind the house. There was no running water. A small bucket of water, a bar of soap and a hand towel were usually available. In the winter months, the large pipe was often frozen shut and one had to go to the toilet armed with a bucket of hot water to open it.

After a while, Fritz returned to our apartment. His face was ashen white, and he seemed totally sober.

"I lost my teeth," he gasped. He had vomited into the toilet and in doing so his upper and lower dentures had followed down the tube.

The party was over for Fritz. He left immediately. We understood the gravity of the situation. Dentures were impossible to obtain in those days.

At about seven the next morning we heard activity in the back of the house. Fritz had arrived. He had brought with him a wooden ladder, several metal buckets and a wooden shoulder bar to carry the buckets. He removed the big square metal lid over the septic tank in the back of the house, lowered the ladder into the bowels of the tank and climbed down, bucket in hand. Up and down he went, filling one bucket at a time. When full, he would carry them to the fortunately large lawn behind the house, where he dumped the contents.

After a few hours' work we heard a jubilant call. "'I found them, I found them!" The teeth had lain on the bottom of the tank about where the big discharge pipe pointed. Fritz cleaned up his tools as well as he could and rushed home triumphantly.

He told us a few days later, brandishing his white teeth, that he brushed the teeth vigorously in hot soap and water, then alcohol, and placed them in a dish of 4711 for two days. 4711 is the name of a German Cologne made in the city of Cologne, at Glockengasse No. 4711.

CHAPTER TEN

CLOSE CALL

It was in the middle of the night on June 5, 1943. The air raid sirens sounded. We got out of bed and slipped into our clothes. There seemed to be more than the usual activity in the sky.

Father said, "I think I should run up to the school."

My Grammar School was located on a small rise, about 100 feet up the street from our house. The large solidly built three story building had a large basement which had been reinforced for use as a bomb shelter for the neighborhood.

Three local residents had been appointed Air Raid Wardens. Their job was to guide the neighbors into the school's bomb shelter in case of an air raid. One such resident was a woman who was a known member of the Nazi Party and who had the reputation of being the neighborhood Nazi spy and informer. Only a few people dared talk with her.

The second one was Mr. Bonnenberg, our next-door neighbor, a sweet and loving man. He was married and had three girls. His wife had been admitted to the hospital that day for delivery of their fourth child which they hoped would be a boy.

The third person was my father.

We looked at the sky, which seemed unusually busy, with lights flashing like lightning here and there. We could hear the hum of airplane engines getting louder and the deep rumble of explosions. The sky began to lighten steadily. High up, a few of what looked like giant candles appeared, slowly drifting towards our neighborhood. Enemy flares attached to parachutes. We called them "Christmas Trees."

"Max," Mother said, "I have a strange feeling about tonight. I think you should stay here and not run up to the school!"

Father stayed.

We heard explosions, very close by.

I had just run down from our second-floor apartment to the ground level to get into the basement, when the apartment door I was passing suddenly opened. I stopped. At the same time the large living room window of the apartment flew across the room, smashing against the opposite wall close to me. All that happened without me hearing any sounds. It was like watching a silent movie. I stood still and looked around at the staircase behind me. Mother was there, hanging onto the stair railing.

I don't know how long it took for me to start to move and to regain hearing again. Mother shouted, "Where is Dad?"

We then heard a voice from the basement "I am down here!" It was Father. Mother and I ran over to the basement door. We could not open it. The whole staircase had shifted.

After a while things quieted down outside. With some pushing and pulling from both sides we were able to partially open the basement door to get Father out.

We heard a weak voice above us. Frau Neef! Frau Neef was in her eighties and lived alone in the third-floor apartment. We ran upstairs. She was OK. She told us that she was hurrying towards her apartment door to go downstairs when the blast came. She saw the door flying towards her. She was able to duck under it and she was unhurt.

Mother told us that she herself was on the way downstairs holding on to the stair railing when suddenly she became airborne. She sailed halfway down the staircase, clutching the handrail. She was unhurt.

After a while things got quiet. I walked outside through our front door which stood open, and onto the street. The surface of our street, which had been black asphalt, was white. I did not understand. Then I saw something black slowly oozing out of a small container. I walked over. It was a small glass ink pot with black ink slowly oozing out. My Grammar School! These same ink pots sat on the students' desks.

I walked up the hill towards the school. On my left I passed a neighbor's house. A small flame was shooting out of the roof. I did not see anybody there.

I got to the school. There was a huge hole in the ground where the front entrance had been. The remains of the adjacent building were hanging over the hole, with small flames and smoke shooting up.

I walked back home. All the windows in our house had been blown out. We were exhausted. We shook the glass out of our bedsheets and crept into bed.

We heard the next day that the bodies of the Nazi woman and of Mr. Bonnenberg had been found at the school, near the crater. Mrs. Bonnenberg had given birth to a boy during the same hour her husband was killed.

My mother had saved my father's life.

CHAPTER ELEVEN

OBERHOF

It was July 1943. Summer vacation was almost over.

We were notified by our school administration in Solingen that there would be no High School taught in Solingen beginning with the new school year in late August.

Both Boys High Schools and the Girls High School would be moved to different locations in central Germany, together with the teaching staff.

For those students refusing to go, there would be no opportunity to continue their education in Solingen.

Shortly thereafter we were notified that our school, the Humboldt School, was being transferred to Oberhof, a resort town in central Germany. Oberhof is a small town in the province of Thuringia, known as the green heart of Germany. The town is known as both a summer and a winter ski resort.

We traveled on a special train, 360 students and teaching staff. Buses took us from the railroad station to our hotel, Hotel Sans Souci, French for "no worries." It was a grand hotel for the period, with a three-story main building with many guest rooms, a number of meeting rooms, and a large dining hall. Outside were beautifully landscaped gardens, flanking a golf course. Ski slopes were within walking distance, with a large international competition ski jump and a smaller practice jump.

I was assigned to a room on the second floor of our hotel, together with two other classmates, Wolfgang Hertel and Wolfgang Standke.

Standke's father was an English teacher and had also come along as one of our teachers.

Our room had one single and one double bunk bed. I was assigned the lower bunk. We had a balcony with a nice view of the gardens. Bathrooms and showers were down the hallway at the other end of the building.

We had two types of administration. One was the school administration consisting of our teachers. The second one was the political administration consisting of a Hitler Youth leader in his early twenties and a few younger adjutants.

That leader oversaw all extracurricular activities including political indoctrination. He was of the classic Arian type. Tall, slender, blond, blue-eyed, handsome and arrogant. I have forgotten his name and will just call him "Leader."

The daily rules were strict. A trumpet call woke us at 6:30 in the morning. Breakfast was served in the main dining hall at 7:30 AM. School started at 8:00 AM. There was no time for a shower, which was a weekend activity. Lunch was from 12:00 to 1:00 PM. School ended in the early afternoon, allowing time for homework. Dinner was served at about 5:00 PM.

Saturday mornings were for room inspection by our Leader. He and his two adjutants would go from room to room in a systematic fashion. Windows had to be spotless, as well as the floors. Fingers were run across the tops of the door frames to check for dust. Bed covers were pulled off to check for wrinkles in the sheets. The bottom sheet had to be perfectly smooth with no creases. We learned that by tying a knot at each corner of a sheet and then forcing the sheet over the mattress, it gave a perfect result.

During mealtime no talking was allowed. Hands had to be always visible and on top of the table. After dinner the Leader took over. The trumpet sounded, and within five minutes we had to be assembled outside in front of the building in uniform, and in columns of three abreast. A few more commands, and we formed into company sizes.

We then marched off the hotel grounds, generally into town, singing Hitler Youth and Nazi Party songs. The weather made no difference. Rain or snow, we marched.

One early evening we were marching through a residential neighborhood with small single-family homes, each with a small nicely landscaped picket-fenced garden in front.

Suddenly we heard the command, "HALT!" We stopped. We were standing in front of a one-story house with a nice flower garden behind a low picket fence.

"PICK FLOWERS!" came the second command. We looked at each other not knowing what to do. "Pick flowers," yelled our Leader again, as he jumped over the fence, starting to pull and tear out flowers in the garden. We followed, and within a minute or two there was nothing left of the garden.

The door to the house opened, and an elderly lady stepped out. "What are you doing? Stop it, stop it!" she yelled. She then started to cry.

The Leader paid no attention to her. He ordered us back into formation, our hands full of flowers. We marched back to our hotel, where we were told to discard the flowers. We were never told what this had been about, and we were afraid to ask.

The "Lights Out" command came at 9 PM in the form of a trumpet sound. No talking was allowed after that. The Leader would often patrol the hallways to listen for anyone talking. If he heard something, the trumpet would sound again.

"Everybody assemble outside in five minutes in full uniform."

We would get dressed and race outside to assemble. We would stand there for perhaps 10 minutes waiting for the next command.

"Dismissed! Everybody back to bed, lights out in five minutes."

Once, we were called out in the middle of the night. It was late fall, cold and raining heavily. We wore our heavy winter uniforms. We stood in the rain at attention for maybe 10 minutes, totally soaked.

Then came the command "Dismissed. Lights out in five minutes."

As soon as we got into bed the trumpet sounded again. "Everybody assemble outside in winter uniform in 5 minutes!"

We began to really hate our Leader.

Over the Christmas Holidays he went on furlough. He left for his hometown of Cologne in West Germany. About two weeks later we got a message informing us that our Leader had been killed during an air raid on Cologne.

Sundays were our days off. We used this time to catch up on things we had to do. I sewed on buttons that had come off shirts; I mended my socks which had developed holes in the heels, sometimes the size of golf balls. One could not buy new socks.

During nice weather we went hiking in the neighborhood hills. Once we found an opening to a cave in a hillside. The opening was about 6 feet wide and almost as high. A small amount of water was trickling out at the bottom.

There were six of us. After some discussion we decided to explore the cave. We had no lights or matches. The cave was a tunnel which for a while continued in a rather straight line. Slowly it seemed to be getting smaller. Piles of rocks were on the ground mixed with increasing amounts of water. I looked back several times. The entrance which at first was shining like a bright large light was getting smaller and smaller. Then came a turn in the tunnel, the piles of rocks got larger, and we were standing in darkness. I thought that if suddenly a portion of the tunnel collapsed and we could not get out, nobody outside would even know where to look for us.

We stopped and whispered to each other. We all felt very uncomfortable. It was time to leave. We turned and slowly walked out. Oh, how good it felt to be able to take a deep breath of fresh air and see daylight again!

During the winter months there was plenty of snow. We often jumped off our second-floor balcony, buried up to our shoulders in the white fluff.

We usually put on our skis at the hotel and walked down the street to the ski slopes in single file. I had a pair of used skis made from hazelnut wood. There were no chair lifts. One had to walk up the side of the slopes to get to the top of the runs.

Once my parents were visiting. They had never seen me on skis. I talked them into walking to the slopes with me so that they could watch me.

It was cold and snowing lightly. I can still see them now. They were standing there, their hands deeply buried in the pockets of their heavy winter coats, their red noses sticking out from under their felt hats, watching me. Between slowly making my way up the side of the slope and skiing down the slope, it took almost one hour. I made one run. My parents had seen enough, they told me.

One day several of us decided to try to jump off the Olympic practice jump. When one came off that jump, one was about 6 feet up in the air. We climbed up several times and had great fun landing on our feet. When I landed on my last jump, only the tip of my right ski came up from the snow. I promptly fell but was not hurt.

The tip of my left ski had broken off. I found it buried in the snow. I took the pieces to a ski repair shop. The man there wrapped the two ends with sheet metal from a vegetable can and nailed and glued the ends.

I could still ski, but the left ski always dragged behind.

CHAPTER TWELVE

BLINDED

It was a beautiful Sunday afternoon, and I was alone in my room.

One of my roommates, Wolfgang Hertel, had left me with some unwelcome presents a month or so before. Hertel was an athlete and musclebound, just the opposite of me. But for reasons I don't recall, we had a playful wrestling match one day in our room.

It resulted in him bleeding from several large flat warts on his hands. Within a few weeks I began sprouting similar warts on the backs of both of my hands, especially my right hand. The biggest wart almost reached the size of a dime, at the base of my right fifth finger.

I had written to my mother about this, and she promptly mailed me some wart medicine which turned out to be a strong acid.

So, that Sunday afternoon, I thought, would be a good time to treat my warts.

The medicine was a clear liquid and came in a one-ounce brown glass bottle capped with a black plastic screw cap. I tried to unscrew the cap a number of times without success. My last try ended with the entire bottle disintegrating in my hands, spilling its contents over my chest and face. I screamed in pain.

I wiped my face and eyes. I could not see. I had no water or faucet close by. After a while the pain lessened, but I was blind. I found my way to the door and stepped out into the hallway. I called out as loud as I could. There was no response. I had to get help. I felt my way along the wall of the hallway, yelling for help and crying. Nobody seemed to hear.

I made it to the staircase and started to feel my way down. I finally heard a voice answering me. Somebody came and took me by the hand, leading me downstairs. I don't remember any details, but my face was washed, and I was put into a car and driven away. After the car stopped, I was guided through a door into a building. A man's voice told me that he was an eye doctor and that he would examine me.

He washed my eyes and face. I had no vision. He covered my eyes with bandages and told me not to remove them. I was so scared. I was blind.

Back at the hotel somebody fed me dinner later. The next day I was taken back to the doctor. My eyes were irrigated, and my bandages were replaced. This routine continued for about a week. Slowly my vision was returning. My bandages were taken off. I began to recognize outlines of objects, but not see them clearly. My doctor told me that I had received chemical burns to my corneas, but that I should continue to improve and that I would be alright.

When my woolen shirt I had worn that day came back from the laundry, the front part over my chest was missing. There was a huge defect with irregular frayed edges.

What a terrifying experience. I had been close to being rendered totally blind.

CHAPTER THIRTEEN

SIMONE

Our dining hall was large, accommodating all the students. The tables were set up in parallel rows, with seating on both sides. The food was prepared and served to us by the kitchen personnel. They were mostly young women in their early twenties. They seemed to be mainly local girls, judging from their accents.

One young woman seemed different. Her hair was black instead of the more common dirty blond. Her eyes were brown instead of the common blue. She appeared friendly but more serious than her coworkers and did not speak much when serving. She had a somewhat sultry deep voice. I found her very attractive and somewhat mysterious.

After a while we exchanged a few words. Her name was Simone. I began to like her and was hoping that she would be serving my food at mealtime. Every few weeks we had a meal I was particularly fond of. Large yeast dumplings, light and fluffy, with a pitted red cherry inside, and a wonderful, sweet vanilla sauce poured over the top. I told Simone how much I liked the dumplings.

The next time she served them she whispered to me that she had saved some extra dumplings for me.

She had them in the kitchen in a little box. I stealthily took them up to my room after dinner.

After a while we started to talk a little. She was nineteen. She was French, from the vicinity of Lyon. She had been kidnapped by a German patrol while walking in town. She had been taken to a large building where other French people were being kept. They were all waiting to be taken to Germany to work there as forced labor. She was shipped to Oberhof and assigned to work in the kitchen at our hotel.

She was not allowed contact with her family in France. She was learning German slowly from her German coworkers. At our hotel she shared a room with a German girl, Frieda. All the full-time employees lived on the third floor of the hotel.

As time went by, I found myself thinking about Simone more. I really liked her; I sometimes woke up at night thinking about her. Once I found myself walking down the hallway in the middle of the night, climbing up the steps leading up to the employee floor, sitting there and hoping she would come down to join me. She never did, of course, and I never told her.

Weeks and months went by, Christmas came and went. Our music teacher and his wife organized interested students into a small orchestra. We performed Hayden's Children's Symphony. I played the snares. It was a success, and we performed several times in town.

Summer was approaching, and with it our six weeks summer vacation. It was 1944. We had been promised to go home to Solingen for the summer, and then return to Oberhof in September.

But something had changed on the war front. The Allies in Europe had launched an offensive against Germany on June 6, 1943, in Normandy, France, and were slowly advancing towards Germany.

Then came the announcement one week before we were planning on going home.

Our vacation to Solingen was canceled. We had to stay in Oberhof. We were terribly upset. Our parents were terribly upset. Word got around very quickly that our parents were coming to Oberhof to take us home for the duration of the vacation, regardless.

Mother came to Oberhof together with a few other parents. I packed only a few clothes. I ran over to the kitchen to say goodbye to Simone. I gave her my address in Solingen and told her that I would be back in 6 weeks.

We got to Solingen without a problem. Nothing had changed. The air raids by the Allies were continuing, but nothing really bad had happened in Solingen since I left.

I received a letter from Simone with a few nice words. The envelope also contained a small twig of the little blue flowers, Forget Me Nots.

I sent her a letter, also including a twig of Forget Me Not which I picked in our garden.

I got one more letter from her with a Forget Me Not in it. I was so anxious to see her again.

Then came the shocking news. We were told that our school would not be returning to Oberhof. We would be reassigned to a little town in Thuringia by the name of Finsterbergen, meaning "Dark Mountain."

Nobody I knew had ever heard of Finsterbergen. We made some inquiries, and the news was not good. It was a small street village in a deeply forested area, with no railroad connection. There were no hotels with anything even similar to our Oberhof hotel.

I decided to wait, to see whether I had other options. But most of my schoolmates, I heard, had decided to go to Finsterbergen.

In any case, I had to go back to Oberhof to collect all my belongings I had left behind.

Mother and I traveled back. The hotel had changed. A girl's high school from Berlin had been moved in. We were not allowed to see our rooms. All our belongings we had left behind had been placed in a big storage room.

I ran over to the kitchen to say hello to Simone. I did not see her. I spotted her roommate, Frieda. "Where is Simone?" I asked her. She hesitated before she answered.

"I don't know," she said. "Simone is not here anymore."

I looked at her for a long time. "Not here anymore? What does that mean?"

She then told me. One day Simone had been very upset. She was seen spitting on Hitler's picture hanging in the hallway. Two days later two men in civilian clothes showed up. They talked to Simone briefly and then took her away. Frieda thought they were GESTAPO, the Nazi secret state police. Nobody in the kitchen dared talk about it

Nobody had seen Simone or heard of her since. She was gone, as if she had never existed.

I was shocked. I did not know what to say. Taken away by the Gestapo.

Had she been upset because she was told I was not coming back to Oberhof? I was her only friend there. What did the Gestapo do to her? Beat her, torture her, kill her?

It was only after the war had ended that the average German heard about the existence of Concentration Camps, where indiscriminate mass killings of interred inmates occurred. The thought of what might have happened to Simone is still too much for me to bear. I will never know.

CHAPTER FOURTEEN

GARDELEGEN

Mother and I arrived back in Solingen with my belongings. What should I do?

My aunt Hetty had returned from Paris and was now living with her boyfriend Karl in a medium-sized town named Gardelegen, about 100 kilometers west of Berlin. My grandmother, Hetty's mother, had packed up and moved to Gardelegen to escape the air raids in the West, and to be with her daughter.

What if I moved to Gardelegen also and went to school there? Hetty said, "Wonderful!"

My grandmother said, "Werner can live with me, and he can go to school there." It seemed like a great alternative to going to Finsterbergen for school. I arrived in Gardelegen by train. Hetty and her friend Karl picked me up and took me to my grandmother's place.

Oma, as I called my grandmother, lived in a small apartment on the fifth floor of an enormous rectangular building in the center of town. One wing of the building housed the city prison. The small apartment where Oma lived was practically under the roof. The windows were at floor level and small. To look out you had to lie on the floor. At certain times of the day, you could watch the prisoners from the jail exercising in the enclosed yard below.

Hetty and Karl lived on the outskirts of town in a private two-story home attached to a factory building, extending deep into the lot in the back, surrounded by a 2-meter-high cyclone fence. The lot was guarded by a beautiful large German Shepherd dog, roaming freely at night, but confined during the day in a large wire enclosure.

School had already started, and I was admitted to a class of my grade without problem. But I found out very quickly that I was not accepted by the boys in my class. I spoke a different dialect, acted differently, and was watched with a mixture of distrust and disdain. I did not make any friends.

Karl's factory was rather interesting. He was an engineer and had designed a two-wheeled trailer for German paratroopers. It was an open trailer with a pole-like bar in front which could be attached to a truck, car, or an animal like a horse, or it could be pulled by hand by two men. It could be launched from a plane by parachute. Karl was producing these trailers as fast as he could for the German Armed Forces. Many years after the war, on a visit to a small town in Normandy France, St. Eglise Sur Mer, I spotted one of those trailers in the local war museum there.

Hetty's German shepherd dog was exceptional. She often took him downtown with her when shopping. On the way back he would carry the shopping basket in his jaws. Even with meat or sausage in the basket he would not stray from his duty. One day Hetty left to go shopping without him. He watched her walking down the street from an upstairs window. Suddenly Hetty heard a commotion behind her. The dog was right behind her. He had jumped through a narrow upstairs window, from the second floor.

After about four weeks in Gardelegen, I decided that it was not the place for me. I hated the thought, but I felt that I had no choice but to join my friends in Finsterbergen.

CHAPTER FIFTEEN

FINSTERBERGEN

I came back to Solingen and notified my school office that I was ready to join my school in Finsterbergen. I packed one large suitcase. My parents and Uncle Otto went to the Solingen Ohligs railroad station to see me off.

The train pulled into the station and stopped. It was packed with people. We ran up and down the platform looking at the cars. It was so crowded, people were standing on couplings connecting the cars, and on steps below the doors, hanging onto handlebars. Most of the doors were closed. What to do? We stopped at the midsection of a car and looked into the window of a compartment. The people inside were seated, three on each side, facing each other. There was a space between the two rows, wide enough for somebody to stand.

Uncle Otto knocked on the window, gesturing to those inside to lower the window so that I could climb in. They decided to ignore us. Uncle Otto got furious. He knocked again, asking them to lower the window. No response. He then picked up my suitcase, swung it over his head, and threw it with full force against the window.

The window shattered into a hail of pieces, showering the people seated inside with glass. There was yelling and cursing. But my suitcase had landed inside. Father and Uncle Otto then lifted me into the car through the window. I stood up between a number of knees and legs. The train started moving. I waved goodbye to my parents and uncle and sat down on my suitcase.

We rolled along for many hours, the cold wind blowing into the compartment. None of the people seated around me talked to me, except for uttering a few curses. The next day I arrived at my destination. I had gotten off the local train in the nearby little town of Lauchroden. I took a bus to Finsterbergen.

Finsterbergen was what one would call a "street village." Basically, a one-street town with only a few houses scattered around and away from the main road. My school had been quartered on property consisting of two buildings. The smaller building facing the street was two stories high, white stucco, and looked quite presentable. There was a larger somewhat shabby-looking two-story wooden building in the back. Behind the building was an expanse of meadows and forest.

Most of the students were housed in the back building. The ground floor consisted mainly of a large meeting room with a wood-burning fireplace. The students' rooms were upstairs. Each had three bunk beds and a *kachelofen* (tile oven) for heat. A *kachelofen* is a solid square structure of brick and glazed tile about three feet in diameter, five to six feet in height, with a flue exiting from the top, venting out through the ceiling. In the front, and behind a cast iron hinged door, is an opening for placing wood or coal, and below is a space for collection of ashes.

Our room also had a small exterior balcony accessible through a narrow-framed glass door. There was a single large movable wooden cabinet for storing clothes and other items.

Our teachers from Oberhof had come along and lived in the front building. Our new political "Leader" also lived in the front. He was a man in his fifties. We had never seen him before. He was almost bald, with a bony body and face, always wearing his brown Nazi Storm Trooper uniform from the early days of the Nazi movement. We did not know his real name, but everybody called him *Knochen* (Bones), since he looked skeletal. Bones always seemed to be in a bad mood. We did not have to do any marching outside or singing. But he was always sniffing around looking for something to criticize.

Meals were served in the large common room downstairs, and classes were conducted there also. The food was OK at first, but nothing close to what we had had in Oberhof. There were no outside activities, except for hiking in the woods on your own.

Slowly winter approached, and the weather got colder, and snow began to fall. Our rooms were cold at night. We asked to use our *kachelofen* for heat. The answer was no. If we wanted to be warm, we should go to the large common room downstairs with the open fireplace.

We were told the motto was ALL FOR ONE, ONE FOR ALL. No exceptions. We pointed out that the front building in which Bones lived, had central heating. That argument fell on deaf ears.

The six of us in our room decided that we had to take things into our own hands. On a cold snowy Sunday, we marched out into the woods, armed with a handsaw we had found. We went to an area where a few pine trees had been felled during the summer. The treetops, each about 6 feet long, had been discarded and left behind. We cut the wood into manageable pieces and dragged them back to our place. We then cut them into 6-to-8-inch lengths and carried them up to our room, where we stacked them outside on our balcony. We had a great little fire every night, with our room a cozy warm.

One day Bones conducted a room inspection. He stuck his nose out to the balcony and spotted our firewood. He blew his stack. We had to carry all our wood downstairs and stack it up in the large common room.

We came up with a different plan. We went back into the woods, dragged the treetops back and cut them up into fireplace sizes. We stacked them on the balcony again. But this time we moved the large clothes cabinet in our room in front of the balcony door and only moved it out of the way to get to the firewood. That way the door was not visible. It worked. We passed the next inspection without any problem. Bones had forgotten about our balcony storage.

We had no radio, but we heard that the war was not going too well. The German armies, and especially the army on the Russian front closer to us, were making what we were told was "strategic retreats."

Our food situation deteriorated. Our main meal began to consist of soup of various types. And then the soup became the same almost every day. Leek soup. Just leeks, with salt and pepper, boiled in water. After a while the smell of boiled leak almost nauseated me. We were told that food was scarce and there was no other food.

We knew that there was a large food locker off the entrance hall of our building, close to a larger enclosed locker holding coal and firewood for the common fireplace. Both were kept locked.

One day the food storage locker had been left unlocked. We opened the door and peered inside. It was packed with canned vegetables and meats we had never seen before. And we were going hungry!

We could not fire up the common fireplace in the meeting room anymore because there was no coal or wood, we were told. But there it was. Lots of coal, lots of wood in the coal bin. We had been lied to all the time. It was being used in the central heating furnace in the front building.

We took some of the coal for our stove. And slowly, that pile became depleted. One day the old man, who was the owner of the building, opened the door to the coal locker and peered inside. We were watching from the staircase nearby. "*Keenen eenen, keenen eenen,*" (not a single piece, not a single piece), he kept saying in his dialect. He was right. All the coal was gone.

CHAPTER SIXTEEN

THE ESCAPE

After an arduous three days on various trains Mother finally arrived. She had to walk to Finsterbergen from the nearest railroad station, which was several kilometers away.

Next to our two school buildings were private homes. Frau Schmitt, the mother of one of my classmates, had rented a one-room apartment next door and lived there so that she could be close to her son. Mother and she had been longtime friends in Solingen, and Frau Schmitt had invited Mother to stay with her, should she come to visit. The two ladies were happy to see each other. No outside visitors were allowed in our camp buildings, so I walked to Frau Schmitt's house to visit with Mother.

Mother told us her story of how she managed to get to Finsterbergen.

Civilian train traffic had been restricted to a radius of 50 kilometers from one's home address. Mother had to travel that distance multiple times to get to me. But she had a plan and was prepared. She had packed several new kitchen knives my father had made.

Before she got on the train she estimated a 50 km radius, where she had to get off. When she had covered that distance, she would get off the train and walk outside the station. She would then find a local lady to whom she would tell her story, about trying to get to her son. The lady would then buy a ticket within a 50 km radius, using her own ID card. Mother would pay her for the ticket and give her one or two kitchen knives as a thank you.

After three days of travel, she arrived in Finsterbergen. After a few days of rest at Frau Schmitt's place, Mother informed me that she had come to take me home. The Russian army in the East was driving the German Army back into Germany, and the American and British armies in the West were moving towards West Germany already. Mother did not want me to fall into the hands of the Russians. She had decided that we should leave as soon as possible and start making our way back to Solingen. She invited Frau Schmitt and her son Klaus to come with us, but Frau Schmitt declined.

It would have been too much an ordeal for her. Frau Schmitt was about my mother's age, around forty-five, but her health was poor. She was a chain smoker with poor blood circulation to her feet and coughed constantly. In addition, she had developed a huge goiter which made her neck look grotesque and which made breathing difficult for her.

I started packing my suitcase. Of course, I had to tell my five roommates about my plans, and I swore them to secrecy. Nobody else would know that I was leaving, I thought. The following day I was packed. Mother and I carried our bags through the woods to the railroad station in the next town, Friedrichsroda.

I had a heavy suitcase and my skis. The station master was gracious and did not ask many questions. We bought two tickets to Erfurt, the next big town, where we would have to switch trains. We left our baggage at the station.

Upon arrival back at camp, Mother said, "Before we go, I have to tell your camp leader that we are leaving."

I was scared of that man. Everybody was scared of him. He was in his fifties, a dyed-in-the-wool Nazi. He always wore his beige Storm Trooper Nazi uniform and highly polished boots. No sense of humor. When he looked at you, you froze. A month before, he had been taken to the hospital with a heart attack. We all prayed that he would die. He did not. He came back, mean as ever.

Mother and I walked upstairs to his office. Mother knocked on the door. "Come in," said a voice. We stepped inside. He stood behind his desk. His right arm shot up into the air.

"Heil Hitler " he shouted.

We stood there staring at him. My mother started talking. "I am Frau Stamm. I came from Solingen to take my son Werner home."

"You came to take your son home? You will do no such thing!" He snarled at us. Mother tried to explain why she came to get me. But he cut her off.

"Werner is staying right here," he shouted. "He cannot leave his post. Werner is the SON OF THE FUHRER!"

Mother bristled. "Son of the Fuhrer? Werner is not the son of the Fuhrer; Werner is MY SON!" she shot back.

His voice became steely cold. "Mrs. Stamm, if you and Werner leave here, I will have both of you arrested," he snarled.

I got scared. Maybe I should stay? That thought shot through my mind.

Mother was silent for a few seconds. Then I heard her voice. "Werner, come, we are leaving."

As we walked towards the door, we heard the shout of "Heil Hitler" behind us. We walked out of the room, Mother slamming the door. We went to Mrs. Schmitt's house. The atmosphere was tense. We had to get up very early in the morning since our train was leaving about 7 AM.

Mrs. Schmitt had one bedroom with one large bed. All three of us crept into the bed, Mother in the middle. But there was no real sleep. Several times during the night Mrs. Schmitt got up to smoke a cigarette, filling the room with smoke. Then we heard airplane engines and noises like explosions and the barking sound of anti-aircraft guns in the distance. We had never experienced that before in the area. We got up at 4 AM, gathered our things, and said thank you and goodbye to Mrs. Schmitt.

As we were walking through the forest, we suddenly heard voices nearby. Here were guys from my school, including my friends. I asked one of them what they were doing there. They had been ordered into the woods to find and pick up any propaganda leaflets dropped by enemy planes, so that the civilian population would not see them.

They were printed in German, three different types, telling the German people about the state of the war.

My schoolmates were told to gather them up but to not read them. They gave me samples to take with me, one of each type. I stuffed them into my jacket. Mother and I made it to the railroad station.

We were not expecting what we saw. The station house stood in flames and people were running in all directions, shouting, trying to put out fires. After a while we spotted the station master. We told him that we had brought our baggage there the day before. He shrugged his shoulders. "All the baggage in the stationhouse is burning," he said, "but there is a small shed over there (he pointed a short distance away) which has some baggage in it." We ran over there, opened the door and, low and behold, there was our baggage, intact.

We left my skis behind and just grabbed my and Mother's suitcases. We asked the Station Master, "Is a train coming?"

"Oh yes," he replied, "and it will be on time."

The train rolled into the station. We got on, and we were on our way to the next big city, Erfurt, where we had to switch trains.

After an hour or so the train slowed to a crawl. We saw a lot of smoke in the distance. Erfurt had been bombed during the night, we were told. As we got closer, we saw flames everywhere shooting from clouds of smoke. The train slowly eased through switches and into the station, where it stopped on a siding. We looked out the window. Fires and smoke everywhere. The large main railroad station house lay in ruins, flames issuing from the rubble.

Someone was shouting, "Everybody off the train!" We climbed down to the tracks, not knowing what to do or where to go. A man told us that there were about three hundred people dead in the bomb shelter underneath the main station building, about 200 feet away. We stood on the rails clutching our bags, looking around. What to do?

There was a single passenger train car sitting on a siding not far from us, apparently empty. Mother said, "Look there!" We made our way to the car. The doors were not locked. The car was empty. We climbed in and sat down. We looked out the window watching the turmoil and confusion outside, wondering what to do. I pulled the enemy leaflets from my pocket and read them. They told things we had never heard of; that the Allies were making rapid progress in the West, pushing back the German forces, and the Russian army was making rapid progress against the German Army in the East. We had always been told that the German army was just making a few strategic withdrawals on the Russian front.

An hour or so passed when suddenly we felt a heavy jolt. Then our car began moving very slowly. A locomotive had hooked up to us. We kept moving, slowly gaining speed, leaving the station. Where were we going?

Mother said, "I hope we are going West and not East where the Russians are." There was no one to tell us. We were the only passengers on the one car train. After about 30 minutes we pulled into a station. Several passenger cars were brought up and hooked to our car. Then passengers started to come aboard. We said nothing and sat still. We did not have any tickets. The train moved on, slowly adding more cars at each stop. Evening came, and we had found out by that time that the train was going West, heading in the right direction for us. Thank God!

After dark, we pulled into a large station. Loudspeakers were blaring, "Everybody out and into the underground air raid shelter. Air attack! Air attack!" Then the wailing sound of Air Raid sirens, which made my flesh crawl.

We were several hundred passengers by that time, pushing and being pushed into the underground shelter. I was thinking about all the dead people in the Erfurt shelter we had just left. We sat for about three hours, waiting. Nothing happened. No bombs fell. All we could hear was the sharp barking sound of 88mm anti-aircraft guns in the distance. After a long while, the air raid sirens gave the wonderfully relieving monotone All Clear sound.

We got out of the shelter and climbed back on our waiting train. It was after midnight by then and the train started moving. Mother and I whispered to each other. It seemed like a miracle that we had gotten away from the camp. The same night that we had planned our escape, a large air raid on the region happened, throwing everything into confusion and turmoil. It was the first air raid ever in that area!

Had we left my camp and gotten on the train without the air raid, we probably would have been found, arrested, and sent to prison.

Was there a guiding hand which had helped us?

CHAPTER SEVENTEEN

MESCHEDE

We rolled along all night. At mid-morning we slowed down to enter a station. The sign said Meschede. It seemed like a small town. We stopped. A few people got off; a few people got on the train. We were sitting there for maybe 10 minutes. Why are we not moving on?

I was sitting by the window, looking out. Suddenly I noticed a commotion outside. The uniformed station master acted strangely. At departure time he normally raises his paddle towards the engine, the green side pointing toward the engineer. Instead, he was running back and forth on the pier, shouting something and waiving his paddle in the air.

He finally dashed forward yelling at the train engineer. The train started to move forward slowly, but it was not gaining speed. It just crawled along at walking speed. We got to the outskirts of town, passing the few last houses, when the train stopped. We were sitting on an about six-foot-high earthen dam above green soggy wet looking flat pastureland. A two-meter-high cyclone fence ran parallel to the dam at ground level.

After a few minutes of nervous silence, a deep humming sound began to fill the air, getting stronger by the second. Airplanes! Then we saw them. A whole swarm of single-engine planes was heading for our train, broadside, at low altitude.

All hell broke loose. Bullets were hitting the train like a hailstorm. People were dropping to the floor screaming. Glass from windows was flying. I slid to the floor next to my mother. Close by, a girl was screaming, "My leg, my leg!"

The planes passed over us, disappearing in the distance. Several of the soldiers on board yelled "Everybody off the train, fast, fast. They will be back!"

I don't know how I got out. I found myself sliding down the embankment on my back, my mother already ahead of me on the ground. In an instant the cyclone fence at the bottom was bent flat to the ground by the sheer weight of the fleeing people.

I suddenly realized that the cap I had been wearing was gone. I looked back up to the train. The cap was lying up there among the rocks. As fast as I could I crawled back up, grabbed it and slid back down the meadow.

I heard my mother yelling, "Werner, Werner!" She was running across the wet meadow toward the houses. I caught up with her. We could hear plane engines again. They were returning.

We ran towards the house closest to us. We heard machine gun fire from the planes. The front door of the house stood wide open, and people were pushing inside. Mother was ahead of me. She made it through the door. As I was about three or four feet from the door, I saw debris and wood splinters raining down in front of me. I looked up. Two large caliber bullets stuck in the door frame just above my head. I made it into the house and jumped down some stairs into the basement where several people had taken refuge already. Mother was there, breathless but alright. We hugged each other and cried.

We sat there for about an hour listening to the commotion outside. There were explosions, close and distant, and much yelling and screaming. Then things got quiet. When we got outside, we looked around, stunned. Several of the homes were burning. People were running in all directions. Some were yelling at us, that all this was our fault because our train had attracted the planes.

Finally, Mother said, "Let's get back to the train."

As we rounded a corner, we saw our train in the open field. The train engine was sitting on its haunches, the front of the engine pointing straight into the sky. Smoke was pouring from the engine. The tracks in front of the train lay twisted. We found our car and our suitcases and carried them to the nearby highway. After about one hour of walking, a German Army truck pulled up. We told the soldiers we had been on our way to Kassel, the next big town. They helped us into the truck where other passengers from our train had already been loaded. About an hour later we pulled up at the Kassel Hauptbahnhof, the main railroad station.

We had to buy tickets for our ride to Solingen. And there we got into trouble, since we were outside the 50 km legal travel range.

"I.D. papers!" demanded the ticket master.

That's where mother came into her own. She was always great at thinking on her feet. "We lost all our papers during the air raid on our train!"

After some back and forth we got our tickets. It was early evening when we disembarked at the railroad station in Solingen Ohligs. We made it! We were home!

CHAPTER EIGHTEEN

HOME AGAIN

I was told that our house was no longer livable. My parents and my favorite grandmother had moved to an apartment house on Richard Wagner Street, about a mile from our house, where Uncle Arthur lived, my mother's twin brother.

My parents told me the story.

It was November 1944. All the cities in our area had undergone massive bombings by the Allies. Only Solingen had been spared. Then one day, a high-ranking Nazi party official gave a speech, praising Solingen as a symbol of the strength and resilience of the German Reich. The following weekend, November 4th and 5th, all hell broke loose. Massive air attacks came at noon time on two successive days, flattening the city.

On the first day my parents were home. Large formations of enemy planes dropped their loads on the city. Father was in the main hallway of our house downstairs when a bomb struck in the vegetable garden across the street. The blast threw Father to the floor, partially burying him under a wall of brick falling on him from the adjacent inside wall. A second bomb hit behind the house next door, creating a huge crater. The back wall of the large three-story house collapsed into the crater, trapping the residents there in their basement shelter. The Bonnenberg family lived there. It took three days for them to be rescued from their shelter. Miraculously, nobody was hurt.

Our house was in bad shape. The roof tiles had all been blown off, leaving the rafters exposed. All the windows were blown out. In several areas interior walls had collapsed. A second-floor balcony, facing the street at my grandmother's house next door, had dropped down to the sidewalk, leaving a gaping hole in the facade.

The day after the first attack, my parents feared that more was to come. They walked to a large underground public shelter about two kilometers away, the same shelter where I had sought refuge several times on my way to school a year before. They decided to spend the night there.

The second attack came again the following noon. There was no German air defense anymore. Our house was vacant. A neighbor saw flames coming from the attic of our house. He raced inside and upstairs to the attic. Using the buckets of water sitting there, he was able to extinguish the flames and save the house. My parents stayed in the shelter for two more days. When they got back, our house and most of the neighborhood houses were damaged but still standing.

The center of the city of Solingen was gone. A large underground shelter in the city center had been hit, and hundreds of residents who had fled there, had died.

The government had also constructed a unique bomb shelter downtown which looked like a large bomb standing on its tail, its tip pointing towards the sky. The exterior wall was concrete, over three feet thick, with no windows. Inside was a circular staircase of concrete. There were several steel doors at its base. This shelter held over three hundred people. Everyone inside was dead. All had suffocated from lack of oxygen, when the city had become a fireball.

Uncle Fritz's house in the city was gone. Fortunately, Uncle was away in the army, and his wife and my cousin Trudi were living in the country with a farmer's family.

If you wanted to walk into the city center, you had to climb over mountains of brick and rubble filling the streets.

This was the situation when I got back from my school camp in Thuringen.

We were living with my grandmother and aunt Hetty in a small one-bedroom second floor apartment in a six-apartment house, a total of five people. Our street cut across a hillside, the houses on one side of the road lying high, and those on our side lying low, above a creek bed. One could walk into the basement from the back of the house.

When looking up the hillside, one would see the large 800-bed city hospital cresting above, with huge painted red crosses on the roofs of the largest buildings.

Food was scarce. I could not apply for food ration cards, since I would have had to report that I escaped from my school camp In Thuringen. I would have been in big trouble. My family carried me along by sharing their food with me.

We heard on the radio that the Allies were slowly but surely moving closer. We were able to listen to the BBC (British Broadcasting Corporation) on short wave on our radio. Those broadcasts were preceded by four deep drumbeats, "Boom Boom Boom Boom," followed by, "This is the BBC London." One had to be very cautious, the radio at low volume, one ear against the speaker, since listening to the enemy was strictly illegal and punishable.

We were slowly being encircled by the American and British armies. During the day, double-tailed American planes lazily cruised overhead at low altitude, looking at the hospital and surroundings, it seemed. There was no anti-aircraft fire anymore.

Occasionally, bombs dropped. When the air raid sirens sounded the alarm, we ran downstairs into the basement of the house and sat there, waiting. At one point, bombs were hitting close to our neighborhood. One of the older neighbor ladies sitting with us freaked out.

"Dear God in heaven, dear God in heaven, help us!" she called out, over and over and over again. She was driving us crazy.

Finally, everybody was yelling at her, "Shut up, shut up!" She quieted down, whimpering to herself.

One small miracle happened in all this mess. My maternal grandmother had become obese with age and was beginning to suffer from congestive heart failure. When she came home from shopping, she had had to stop and rest on the first staircase landing before proceeding to her apartment on the second floor. With less food to eat and running up and down the stairs during air raids, she had lost all her excess weight and was able to negotiate the stairs without slowing down. She was feeling great and her "heart asthma" was gone.

Our closest public shelter was up the street and consisted of a 6-foot diameter tunnel underneath an elevated railroad track. A three-foot diameter water main ran through the tunnel. We would often run up there when the air raid sirens sounded and sit on the water main. Once, a bomb fell close to the entrance to our shelter, hitting the water main outside. A neighborhood teenage girl in the tunnel was sitting on the pipe right next to a valve. The valve partially blew off in the blast, pinning her thigh under. A huge geyser of water erupted, dousing everybody. We got the screaming girl out from under the valve and scrambled out of the tunnel as fast as we could.

A group of Italian prisoners of war were brought in to fill the crater after the water main had been repaired. I still remember watching them, mainly leaning on their shovels, talking and laughing instead of working. The war had ended for them.

It was kind of ironic that our former Italian Allies under Mussolini had now become our adversaries under their new Western Allied commander. We knew that when the Italian army was still our ally, the German army often had to come to rescue the Italians from difficult situations. It was said that the Italian tanks had five gears. One forward and four reverse.

Our own house was in bad shape. Nobody lived there anymore, but most of our belongings including furniture were still there. My parents and I walked there every day to start cleaning up. We were able to get some plastic sheeting to close the blown-out windows. Glass was not available. Sometimes we slept in our beds. One night it was raining heavily. Although we lived on the second floor of a three-story building, water was dripping from the ceilings everywhere, including onto my bed. I found an umbrella which I hung over my bed so that I was partially protected from the rainwater dripping down on me.

The first priority was to stop the rain from coming in. There were no roof tiles to be bought. My job was to gather as many tiles as I could find in the neighborhood, and to carry them up to the roof. Many tiles were lying on the attic floor, still intact. Many were lying in the backyard, partially covered by dirt from the large crater next door, where a bomb had gone into the septic tank. I also gathered all intact roof tiles from the neighbor house, which had partially collapsed. I climbed up into the roof and attic to find intact tiles. Father was busy installing roof tiles on our house and laying brick to close big holes in interior walls. I picked up bricks from next door, which I then had to clean from mortar so Father could use them.

We worked hard every day, all day long, to at least make our apartment livable again. And then finally the day came when we could move back home.

CHAPTER NINETEEN

APRIL 1945, SOLDIER FOR A DAY

We heard on the news that our area had been surrounded and totally encircled by the Allied forces. It was a large circle, which included the entire Ruhr district, producing all the coal in Germany, also including the heavy armaments industry.

There were some desperate last-minute attempts to stave off the inevitable.

Richard Schmitt was our neighbor living two houses up the street from us. His job was making manicure instruments in a nearby factory. One day he was told by the local authorities that he was drafted into the Volks Sturm, a newly created organization, the "People's Storm," to defeat the enemy. The organization consisted of older men not fit for the draft.

Together with three other older men from the neighborhood, Richard's group was outfitted with a small four-wheeled pull cart, a single rifle, and a handful of bullets. Uniforms were not available. The four men were told to march to a certain point on the outskirts of Solingen, near the ancient castle of Schloss Burg, and to engage the enemy there.

Richard told us more than a year later what happened that day. They were dutifully slugging along on the road towards their destination, when they were stopped by an American jeep patrol. They immediately raised their arms in surrender and handed over their rifle. They were taken prisoner and then shipped off to a prisoner-of-war camp, about 100 miles away. Once there, Richard was ordered to work as a cook in the camp kitchen. He had never cooked anything in his life before.

Life was good in the camp. He told us later that he could not believe the terrible waste of precious food he witnessed there. The camp was assigned a certain amount of food every month, which was way too much for the prisoners to consume. Instead of having a lesser amount of food delivered, the American camp commander ordered all the excess cases of food incinerated, every month, in a mountainous pile. The German civilian population was starving from lack of food at the same time.

After one year, Richard was discharged from the prison camp, and he returned home.

CHAPTER TWENTY

HORSE TRADING

From what we could see as civilians, what was left of the German Army was in total disarray.

One afternoon, my friends and I were hanging out at the local bakery, Heinen, in our neighborhood, hoping for a handout of bread or cookies. As we were sitting outside on the sidewalk, a beautiful 2-door Adler coupe automobile pulled up, painted in Army Green camouflage colors. Two Army officers got out, in immaculate uniforms and tall shiny boots. Instead of entering the bakery, they started to walk down the street on the sidewalk. We were watching them until they disappeared in the distance. We waited for them to return. They did not come back. We tried the doors of the car. They were not locked. There were no keys.

The following day we ran back to the bakery to check. The car was sitting there, just like we had left it. We never saw the officers again. After a few days, the wheels were missing, interior items had been taken out, and the beautiful car slowly became a wreck. I had tried to talk my father into moving the car to our place, to store it in the chicken house, but he said that would amount to stealing from the government and he was afraid to do that.

Since the German Army abandoned their motorized vehicles because of lack of fuel, they requisitioned horses and carts from the local farmers. Columns of soldiers were now walking along slowly on the main road in the city in both directions, with horse-drawn wagons. It seemed that nobody knew where they were going.

Uncle Arthur told us that soldiers were trading army horses for civilian outfits. He had obtained a beautiful three-year-old Army horse for a pair of old pants and a shirt. A neighbor of his had also gotten himself a horse. But instead of walking it home, he was on his bicycle, leading the horse along the road. Suddenly, the horse bolted, pushed him and his bicycle into a roadside ditch, and took off. He never saw the horse again.

Uncle Arthur led his horse down to the back of his house, and through the door into the large basement room. He called a local butcher he knew. The butcher shot the horse and butchered it for a portion of the meat. Meat was a very precious commodity in those days. My mother came with all the canning jars she could find, and we canned horse meat for several days. I felt very sorry for the beautiful horse but at least we had meat to eat. I still did not have any ration cards to buy food for myself. We took much of the canned meat home to our house. It lasted us for more than one year.

CHAPTER TWENTY-ONE

THE AMERICANS ARE HERE

With all this confusion, life continued.

Uncle Otto, who had lost his house in the city, lived next door now, and walked to work every day. One day, shortly after leaving for work, he came running back shouting "The Americans are here, the Americans are here!"

We rushed to ask him, "Where are they?"

"Up on Main Street, with lots of tanks," he reported.

We did not hear any shots being fired. "Where is the German Army?" I asked.

"I don't know," he said. "I did not see any German soldiers."

We kids looked at each other. Main Street was only a couple of hundred yards away. "Let's run up there and see!"

We got there, and our mouths stood open. Yesterday the German army with their horse-drawn wagons had been moving up and down Main Street in both directions. Today we only saw a long column of tanks slowly moving up the street. But they were not German tanks. They had white stars painted on the side. The front ends were covered with large pink sheets. In the open turret of each tank stood a helmeted soldier, looking straight ahead. And he was black. His face, his hands were black.

We had never seen a black person before. They were black soldiers. We just stood and stared. We did not know what to do. The column seemed endless. No shots were fired. The war was over for us. "The Americans are here, the Americans are here!"

We ran home after a long time watching. We turned on the radio. There was fighting going on in northern and southern Germany, as well as to the east of us. But for us the war was over. Solingen was within the circle the Allies had closed. No more air raids. We could sleep at night. It was such a relief; it was hard to describe. The war was over, and everything would be OK now. Or so we thought.

CHAPTER TWENTY-TWO

THE VACUUM

The German government was no longer in existence. The American occupation forces had taken over. But had they?

All Nazi party members were relieved of their jobs. The problem was that those party members had been the ones in charge of all functions of not only government, but all civic responsibilities, and commercial activities as well.

We found this out almost immediately. During the war, there were many foreign prisoners of war who had been transported to Germany to fill jobs normally held by Germans. They were kept in labor camps. One such "camp" was a restaurant and pub in our neighborhood, with an attached bowling alley. The prisoners had bunks for sleeping set up in the bowling alley, and food was prepared and served in the attached restaurant. On weekends, the kids from the neighborhood often walked over there and stared at the prisoners walking around, behind a two-meter-high wire fence. Many were Russian, some were Polish. There were a few German guards, generally older men not fit for serving at the front. The prisoners were released immediately by the American authorities. They were free to roam around the city and neighborhoods.

Very soon the problems started. Almost every night after dark, we could hear women screaming. We heard that many German women were being attacked and raped by the former prisoners roaming the streets. Since there was no longer a German police force, there was nobody to turn to.

The Allies had decided that the foreign former prisoners were entitled to decent private living accommodations. A large block of modern three-story apartment buildings in the Mangenberg district, spared from the bombings, was ordered cleared of the residents living there. They were allowed to take with them only personal belongings they could carry. Hundreds of former prisoners moved in. Some months later, when repatriation of those people had begun, and the apartment houses became vacant, the interior of the houses could be inspected. There was almost total destruction of the former residents' furniture and other belongings. Even the wooden staircase railings between floors had been ripped out.

We heard later that the majority of the Russian prisoners at first refused to be repatriated to Russia. Even though they had been prisoners of war in Germany, their lives had been immeasurably better than in Russia under Stalin. And they had seen how German people lived. But under the Yalta Agreement between the Allies, the Russians had to be shipped back to their homeland. We heard years later that most of those men were executed by Stalin after their return.

The food situation became a disaster. We were issued new ration cards which were calculated in calories, something we had never heard of. The standard daily allowance for an adult was 1000 calories. Coal miners were at the top of the list with an allowance of 3000 calories. 1000 calories for our family was severe. My father worked hard all day in the factory producing household knives. At breakfast, Father and I sat across from each other at the table, looking at two slices of bread for both of us. There was no butter, just homemade fruit jelly. No real coffee, but a brew looking like coffee, from roasted barley. No cold cuts, no meat, no cheese, no cereal.

People were saying, "During the war, Hitler gave us vitamins (vitamin C). From the Americans, we are getting calories. When are we going to get something to eat?"

After a small lunch at home, Father was usually so exhausted, he often leaned back on the couch where he sat and went to sleep, something he had never done before. Mother always got upset. She did not understand that he was too weak to work.

At one point we were out of potatoes, our main staple. Mother went to the neighbors in our house asking whether she could have their potato peels. In those days, potato peels were razor thin, you could almost read the newspaper through them. Mother made potato peel soup. At first it seemed tolerable. But after a few meals of that, the smell of cooking potato peels began to get to me, to the point that I was getting nauseated.

But there was food to be had, we heard. There was a thriving Black Market. Anything was available, but you had to pay 10 times the regular price. Most people, including our family, did not have that kind of money.

There was only one way to cope with the hunger.

CHAPTER TWENTY-THREE

HAMSTERN

A hamster is a small rodent which packs food into its cheeks before running to store it in a safe place. In the German language, "hamstern" is a verb with a similar meaning.

The three of us sat together. "We cannot go on like this," Mother said. "I think we have to go hamstern to get some food on the table."

We all agreed. But how? Father said, "But I have to work to make money!"

Mother said, "Then I will go." We had no idea how she was going to do that. She asked Father to make her some kitchen knives of various types and sizes, to exchange for food. She did not exactly know where to go, but she said that Oldenburg in Northern Germany was an area with lots of farms. And farmers had food.

Oldenburg is a large agricultural area maybe 200 or more kilometers north of Solingen. Father made the knives, and Mother packed up and got on her way. In Solingen Ohligs, she got on a train heading north. We did not hear from her for several days, but after a week or so she was back. And she was loaded up with food.

Actually, "hamstern" was illegal, since theoretically, it was taking food away from the regular distribution channels. On the other hand, you could not find food to buy with your food ration coupons either.

Mother came home with bacon, eggs, flour, and other things we could not get normally. She told us that on the way back to Solingen, the railroad police checked her baggage at an Oldenburg railroad station. She was told to open her large bag. She had hidden a side of bacon behind the inner lining of the bag. As the policeman put his hand inside the bag to check its contents, Mother slid her hand into the bag also, next to his, so that he became very uncomfortable, and pulled out his hand. She passed the inspection. We were elated. The food she brought home lasted almost a month.

Then Mother said, "Max, it's your turn now!" Reluctantly, Father readied himself. He was not a "people person" like Mother was. Instead of a train, he mounted our family bicycle and took off. After almost a week he was back, totally exhausted and emaciated.

Mother said, "What did you get?" Father pointed at the back of his bike. There was a bag of potatoes, maybe 50 pounds. "That's it?"

He told a sad story. On the road west to Dusseldorf, he came across a friend from Solingen, going home. He also was on a bicycle. But he had a problem with air leakage from one of his tires. Father let him borrow his hand pump and the man took off.

Father crossed the Rhine River and pedaled into the countryside. He stopped at a number of farmhouses, but nobody was interested in his knives. He finally talked one farmer into selling him a bag of potatoes. In those days farmers were so flooded with things in exchange for food, it was said that the floors of their cow barns were covered with Persian Rugs. Father gave up after he got the potatoes. On the way home, about 10 miles from Solingen, his rear tire went flat. He had to walk the bicycle home. "I will never go hamstern again," he stated.

Things were not good at home. Electricity was intermittent, and then it became rationed. Some people knew how to get around that. The line voltage was 220V. If you disconnected one of the two hot wires coming into the meter and connected a ground wire instead, the line voltage dropped to 110V. The Solingen streetcars had a line voltage of 110V for their light bulbs. Pretty soon, many of those bulbs disappeared. The electric meter in your house did not turn when you turned on the low voltage lights. So, you had light, and saved money on electricity. Cooking was done with gas.

There was no water for several weeks, after the water main had burst. We had a natural spring in our neighborhood which became the only source of water for us, about one half mile down a walking path, below a cluster of older homes, called Stockdum 2. I took many trips to the spring, equipped with various containers, to join the neighbors standing in a bucket line.

The time came again to procure food. Mother said to me, "You are coming with me this time. I need your help carrying the food." We got on a train, going north, equipped with sandwiches to carry us over. Mother had never traveled that route before. After a few hours, the train stopped.

"End of line," came the announcement over a loudspeaker. We got off. The train had stopped close to a bridge over a good-sized river. The bridge was lying largely in the water, attached to the shore on only one side. It was a war casualty. We had to balance our way across on wooden planks, which had been laid on the bridge girders. There was no train on the other side, just a two-lane highway close by. We started walking, together with all the other train passengers. It seemed like we walked forever, all afternoon and into the early evening. Periodically, we were passed by British Army trucks. I remember them having a very high ground clearance, with a small cab up front, making a high-pitched whining noise when passing. We raised our thumbs into the air to perhaps catch a ride, but of course had no luck. After hours of walking, we finally reached a small town. The road ran through its center, lined on both sides by homes. Something was different, though.

Everything looked normal on the right side. On the left side, a 10-foot-high wire fence ran between the road and the homes. Behind the fence were many angry looking adults, mainly men, shouting in a foreign language and waving their fists at us. Word got around that those people were foreigners, mainly Poles, who had been freed from their labor camps and released into the community, but then assigned to live in private homes, after the German owners had been ejected. A tall fence had been erected around those homes to protect the German residents in the neighborhood.

We felt scared looking at those people. We got past the little town with a sigh of relief. There were only a few farmhouses after that. It was getting dark. We stopped at one farmhouse and asked if we could stay overnight. The people graciously let us sleep in the hay barn after giving us a bowl of hot milk with chunks of dry bread thrown in.

The next morning, we walked on, but soon realized, after offering our knives at several farms, that this exercise was totally futile. We turned around and walked back to the river and across to the train station. We took the next train out. When we got home the only thing we brought with us was a leftover sandwich which Mother had made before we had left home.

"I will never take you again," she said. "You bring me bad luck!"

CHAPTER TWENTY-FOUR

TO KILL THE GOOSE

After we had consumed the potatoes, father had brought back from his trip, we were totally out again. Being without potatoes is for a German like being out of rice for an Asian.

A total of six families lived in our three-story house. The large basement was divided by wooden slats into six compartments, one for each family. The slats were spaced about 2 inches apart, to allow for air circulation. The separate basement compartments for each family were used to store food, coal for the stove, potatoes, and other items.

The largest common room was the separate laundry, which held six portable metal bathtubs, and six hand-operated wooden tub washing machines, each with a wringer mounted on the hinged lid on top. In the corner of that room sat a built-in wood or coal fired stove for heating the water for the laundry. The bathtubs were stored in the basement for their once weekly use, when each had to be carried upstairs to an apartment for the Friday evening hot bath. Each apartment had a single cold-water faucet in the kitchen. One obtained hot water by heating cold water in a large container on the kitchen stove.

Each family had the use of the laundry room for one week, in rotation, once every six weeks. The wet clean laundry would be carried in a basket up five floors to the attic, where clotheslines had been strung. It often took close to one week for the laundry to dry when the weather was cold. In the winter, the clean washed clothing would often be frozen stiff, so that one could break a frozen shirt in half. If one needed an item which was wet or frozen one would take it off the line and dry it in the apartment. Doing laundry in the basement during cold winter days would create such a dense fog from the hot water, there was zero visibility. We had to shout to communicate with each other.

Home canned food in glass jars was stored on shelves. Piles of coal for cooking and heating were kept in open bins, potatoes in wooden crates. After the September potato harvest each family would store several hundred pounds of potatoes in crates for the winter months.

Well, we were out of potatoes again, after we had consumed Father's prize.

One day Mother came up from the basement producing a large potato from her apron. "Look what I found in front of our basement gate!" she said.

The three of us looked at the beautiful large potato. "It was just lying there, right outside our gate," she said. We could not believe it.

Who had dropped it? Should we ask the other tenants if they perhaps dropped a potato?

Mother said "No, not a good idea. We would have to give it back. But now we have a potato." We agreed. We greatly enjoyed eating that potato.

A few days later another big potato lay in front of our gate. Mother picked it up and brought it upstairs. We greatly thanked whoever dropped it there. And then there was another! We did not know what to think. And it kept going like this for several weeks. We said nothing to anybody.

One day Mother said, "I see rat doodles in our basement. I have to get some poison to kill that rat." A few days later, she said, "I'd better start looking for the dead rat before it starts to smell up everything." Mother looked everywhere. She turned around an empty wooden crate which laid on its side.

There was the rat, dead, lying inside the crate on a large pile of beautiful potatoes. The rat had apparently stolen them from the neighbors' compartments and stored them in our compartment. The large ones, which we had found outside our gate, had been too big for the rat to get between the slats of the gate.

We all felt like crying. We had killed the goose that laid the Golden Egg!

CHAPTER TWENTY-FIVE

AMERICAN OCCUPATION

Life slowly changed to a different and new normal state. The American Army occupied Solingen, as well as most of West Germany. Their Solingen headquarters were on the Germanen Strasse, a beautiful tree-lined street with upper-class two-story single-family villas on both sides. This area had escaped bomb damage for some reason. The owners of the homes had been told to leave, and American Army officers were moved in. No German civilians and no civilian traffic were allowed on the street. At one end, an Army checkpoint was set up in the Wasserturm Restaurant, which soon also became a trading center for German citizens and American soldiers.

I made many trips there to get cigarettes for my father, mainly Camel cigarettes, which he liked best. Of course, they came at a price, and kitchen knives were not wanted. One day I took our Voigtlander single lens reflex camera, the only camera we had. I got 200 cigarettes, which in those days were worth about $2.00. Father was delighted. He could not function without nicotine.

In our garden, Father was growing his own tobacco plants. When the leaves had reached a certain size, he cut them and dried them in the kitchen oven. I had to then slice them into thin strips and roll them into cigarettes in cigarette paper, for him to smoke. A few times he got hold of Russian Machorka, but that was too strong even for him. One could see German men walking around town with walking sticks sporting a sharpened nail tip at the business end. When spotting a discarded cigarette butt on the ground, it was carefully speared, and the butt would quickly disappear into the jacket or pants pocket of the new owner. Five butts made one new cigarette. And, of course, you did not discard that butt either.

We did not see much of the American presence in our daily life. Once we were told that an Army patrol would come to our neighborhood to check for guns or other contraband, which we were not allowed to have. My grandfather had owned several hunting rifles, which now, many years later, were hanging on a wall in the factory as souvenirs.

We tossed those into the septic tank. In anticipation of the inspection, I also set on the piano a piece of sheet music with Sousa's American marching song, "Under the Double Eagle." The cover sheet showed a big American flag. The American soldiers paid absolutely no attention to it and instead asked about cameras and watches. We had nothing to give them.

Uncle Willi, my father's older brother, asked my father to establish together with him a company producing cutlery. Uncle Willi would run the business end, my father would make the knives. They argued about the name, "Willi and Max Stamm" versus "Max and Willi Stamm." I preferred the latter, since that name would roll off the tongue easier. Willi won.

Since food was still in very short supply, Uncle Willi decided that, as a businessman, he would be able to procure food for our families. He took a train into the countryside. A week later he was back, beaming. "Three big wooden crates filled with all kinds of food are on their way," he announced. "They will be arriving at the train station Solingen-North."

We waited a few days before going to the station to inquire. Nothing. We went every day after that. Still nothing. The crates never arrived. Or if they did, they were probably kept by the train station personnel who must have gotten very curious about our intense interest in that shipment from the countryside.

CHAPTER TWENTY-SIX

HENRY THE ROOSTER

Since food was in short supply, even a year after the war ended, we had to think of ways to feed ourselves.

We lived on the outskirts of town. Each of the tenants in our house had been assigned a garden plot, on a piece of land adjacent to the house. My grandmother, whose property it was, also had an orchard with about 20 fruit trees of various types. Those were hers. Although we were family, we had to buy the fruit, apples, pears, plums, cherries, or apricots from her. She also sold fruit to the neighborhood. Even fallen and bruised fruit was sold at a discount.

Mother and I worked our garden plot, growing potatoes, bush beans, pole beans, carrots, rhubarb and many other vegetables. There were no insecticides. To reduce damage from insects, we set out little flat dishes with machine oil at intervals, and many of the little critters found their end by jumping into the little dishes.

In early spring, with the ground still partially frozen, we opened the septic tank behind the house, filled buckets with the sewage and carried them down into the garden where the liquid was poured out over the planting beds. After a few heavy rains the sewage would slowly disappear into the earth and become fertilizer. Pieces of disintegrating newspaper would still lay testimony to the origin of the fertilizer.

We also supplemented our menu with meat and eggs from our small farm. We had rabbits in small cages. They were my charge. I had to cut grass for them daily for food. Once a week I cleaned out the cages. The waste would go on the manure pile which mainly held waste from the chickens and from Lotti, our sheep. We had about ten or so chickens, White Leghorns, which were of large size, headed by a single large rooster. Henry was his name. He and my father were best friends.

When Father took his daily breaks from work in the factory, he would walk into the orchard. Henry would fly up and land on Father's shoulder. The two of them would then slowly walk through the orchard looking at things. When it was time for Father to get back to work, Henry would land back on the ground and go on his way to look after his chickens.

Uncle Otto, who lived downstairs, acquired a car, a Hanomag. It was a tiny post-war automobile which barely held four people. The exterior door panels were made of stiffened cardboard. One could slice them with a knife. I once watched Uncle trying to take his family for a ride. Our street was on a moderate incline. Uncle was going to drive. His three passengers squeezed in, and the doors closed. Uncle started the engine and apparently let out the clutch. The car jumped up and moved forward slightly. The engine stopped. He tried again. The car hopped and stopped. After a heated discussion inside the car the passengers climbed out and walked up to the top of the hill. This time Uncle Otto was able to let out the clutch without killing the engine. He slowly drove to the top of the hill. The three passengers got back in, and the car drove away.

Uncle Otto had one problem. There was no garage for his car. He approached my father. Could he park in the chicken house in the backyard? The chicken house was large, about 10 feet high, with a big double door, and with generous space inside. It was big enough to accommodate the little car. Father agreed.

But Henry the Rooster had not been consulted. With the barn doors open, Uncle could drive into the chicken house. But walking away or walking to the chicken house became a challenge. When Henry spotted Uncle Otto, he would run and then fly at him with full force, hacking at him. My father shrugged his shoulders. What could he do? Uncle Otto suggested killing the rooster. Father disagreed. Uncle Otto finally succeeded in getting to or from his car by carrying a big stick, which he kept swinging wildly at the approaching Henry.

CHAPTER TWENTY-SEVEN

LOTTI

Lotti was our sheep. Since milk was almost impossible to buy after the war ended, we decided to get our own supply by acquiring a Dutch Milk Sheep.

We bought a little lamb and housed it in a small shed which I built next to the rabbit hutch. It took patience, though, to wait until the lamb could produce milk. When Lotti was old enough to get to maturity, I loaded her into a four-wheeled hand wagon and took her to a local farmer. The ram there was delighted to meet Lotti and promptly impregnated her. It took a few months before Lotti had two babies. After they had grown enough to be weaned, we sold the babies.

We had Lotti to ourselves. But nobody in the family had ever milked a sheep. We found an old neighbor lady who knew how. She came over once a day, sat down beside Lotti and milked her. She produced about a quart a day of delicious milk. But the lady insisted on keeping half of the milk for herself.

I watched her a number of times milking Lotti. We decided that we could really use a full quart a day for ourselves. Mother volunteered to milk Lotti, since she had milked cows during her teenage years. But things didn't go very well. Mother did not have much patience with Lotti, who sometimes kicked her. Mother then pinched her utter, which in turn was not appreciated. It was the last straw for Mother when one day Lotti kicked the milk bucket, knocking it over and spilling its contents.

It was my turn. Lotti and I were good friends. I practiced carefully without hurting her, and soon she was happy, and I was happy. No more problems. We had our daily quart of milk. Lotti got along fine with Father also. Sometimes when he was standing in the orchard gazing at the trees, Lotti would sneak up from behind, then take a run at him, ramming the back of his knees, which at one time caused Father to fall backwards and on top of her.

I took walks with Lotti in the orchard. One day, when the apples were getting ripe, I decided to eat an apple, which of course belonged to my grandmother. Lotti had been staked out underneath the apple tree. I climbed up into the tree so that I could not be seen by anybody. Lotti could not reach the apples from below. But she was clever. She walked forward to the end of the chain. She then kept walking forward on her hind legs, using the chain as a lever to pull her upright into a standing position, where she could reach the apples.

One day Lotti and I were enjoying eating apples together. My grandmother spotted Lotti standing upright. She hurried into the orchard, yelling at the top of her voice. When she reached Lotti, she bent down and pulled Lotti's stake out of the ground. That caused Lotti to fall forward on her front legs. Lotti took off, racing across the orchard. Grandmother fell forward but kept hanging on to the chain, and was being dragged around, cursing and screaming. Father, in the factory nearby, heard the noises and came running to see what had happened. He ran over to his mother and made her let go of the chain.

She was lying there yelling and cursing, all scraped up. Father helped her up and walked her back to the house, trying to calm her down. I waited for quite a long time before I decided it was safe for me to climb down from the tree, unnoticed.

And I waited for about two weeks before I broke the story to my father.

CHAPTER TWENTY-EIGHT

THE HONEST THIEF

We had about eight chickens giving us fresh eggs daily. Inside the chicken house, I had built eight wooden boxes in a double row, each outfitted with a comfortable layer of hay to create a nest for a chicken to sit and lay an egg. And for a special enticement, just in case the chicken was not too bright, I had placed into each nest a porcelain egg. Porcelain eggs look like regular white eggs. I bought them at a feed supply store. Chickens were more likely to sit on a nest with an egg in it, than on an empty nest.

I was on good terms with my chickens. I fed them grain every day, and worms when I was working in the garden. When I was digging up a garden bed for planting, they would be at my side watching for a worm to come up. Sometimes a chicken would ride on my working shovel waiting for a treat.

Egg laying went on at different times during the day but was usually finished by late afternoon. At about five or six in the afternoon I would collect the freshly laid eggs, leaving the porcelain eggs behind. I would then lock the door to the chicken coup and carry the eggs home.

One morning when walking to the chicken house to unlock it, I noticed the door standing wide open, and the chickens roaming about outside. The outside padlock had been broken off and was lying on the ground. I stepped inside and looked around. Everything looked alright except for one thing. The eight porcelain eggs were gone! I had to laugh to myself. I tried to picture the thief's face when he realized what he had brought home. I did not replace the lock immediately.

Two days later, the porcelain eggs were back in their nests, as if they had never left.

CHAPTER TWENTY-NINE

BACK TO SCHOOL

It was September 1945. School had started again. But things had changed.

Solingen had always had three high schools. Two boys' high schools, and one girl's high school, the August Dicke School. The two boys' schools had survived the war, but the girl's school had suffered severe bomb damage and could not re-open. The students from the girls' school were assigned to my school, the Humboldt School.

There was one serious problem, though. How do you keep the sexes apart in one school building? The wise education authorities found a solution. They decided to split teaching periods into half day periods, one half day for girls, one half day for boys. Boys would start school at 8 AM and end at 12 Noon. Girls would start at 1 PM and finish at 5 PM. This schedule would alternate every week.

In order to absolutely avoid any chance of contact between the sexes at changeover times, the morning students would exit at noon through the front door of the building, while the afternoon students would wait to enter at the rear door, after the morning students had left. There was no such thing as dating between students. One male student was expelled for dating a girl who was not even a student at the school.

The faculty had also changed. Our new math teacher was Emil Ruckes. He was a jovial, middle-aged, rotund man who liked to talk about his family, and especially his small granddaughter, Marlene. He would play hide and seek with her, stepping behind a tree with his big stomach sticking out, calling out, "Marlene child, come and find me?"

In class, he was more serious. When a student did not come up with an answer quickly enough, he was whacked over the head with a 12-inch ruler. I happened to own a quarter inch thick sturdy wooden ruler with a thin metal edge on one side, which Mr. Ruckus liked best. I never got whacked, maybe because I owned the ruler.

Then there was Kanditer, our geography teacher. Nobody seemed to know his real name. Kanditer was very short-tempered. He always sported, in his left hand, a huge bundle of keys, which must have held the keys for every lock in the school. When you did not come up with the right answer to a question, you had to duck quickly to avoid the keys flying towards your head.

Once, I was standing up front in class, before a huge map of Italy. "Show me the City of Trieste," Kanditer demanded.

I looked at the map. I saw the name but thought it should be pronounced "Triest."

He had said, "Tri-est." Before I knew it, I saw the bundle of keys heading for my head. I was able to duck just in time.

Our Latin teacher was Mr. Bohmhammel. We had never heard of a name like that. We decided to call him "Bommel" for short. He seemed very different from all the other teachers. We never saw him smile or laugh. He walked tall and very stiffly, with his head slightly tilted forward. You could always locate him by just listening. "Ahem." He was constantly clearing his throat. While lecturing or explaining something at the blackboard, he would go "Ahem." Pretty soon, the whole class would join in "Ahem, Ahem." Bommel would not react, except for one time, when Ernie got his goat.

Ernie was a classmate with straw-blond densely curled hair, who sat alone in a front bench. The heavy wooden benches were built for two students and consisted of a single unit of desk with seats attached.

Bommel was talking and stopped to do a few heavier than normal "Ahems."

Ernie responded with a salvo of "Ahems." Bommel turned towards Ernie, grabbed him by his dense hair and tried to pull him out of his bench. Ernie held on, Bommel kept pulling, with the end result that the entire bench went upside down, with Ernie pinned underneath. We all rushed to get Ernie out from under and put the bench back into its normal position. That done, Bommel went "Ahem," and continued with his lesson as if nothing had happened.

One day, with Bommel lecturing up front, I noticed a fly lazily circling over my head, then landing right in front of me on my desktop. The fly slowly walked about on the desk, first this way, then that way. I was watching closely. I had always found it challenging to catch flies. With my left hand open and totally concentrating, I very slowly advanced towards the unsuspecting insect. One swift movement, and I had it in my closed left hand. While contemplating my catch, I suddenly realized that it had gotten very quiet in the classroom. I looked up, and right into Bommel's stern face staring down at me. He was standing right before me. I then realized that the entire class was also looking at me. I froze for a few seconds. I still had the fly. What to do?

I opened my hand, very, very slowly. I watched the fly walking out, looking dazed, then slowly taking to the air, in a lazy upward spiral, my eyes following. The entire class broke into laughter, Bommel went "Ahem," while I sat there, frozen. Bommel turned, walked back to the front of the class, and resumed his lecture. He did not say a word. I really appreciated Bommel for the first time.

Mr. Brendel was one of the younger teachers, about thirty-five-year-old. He taught French. He was generally liked by us, and he sometimes told us World War II stories during class.

He had been a soldier serving in a motorized '88 anti-aircraft gun unit on the Russian front. He proudly told us how his unit had shot off many advancing Russian tanks by leveling their feared and highly effective guns horizontally at the tanks.

CHAPTER THIRTY

NEW STUDENTS

Our class had shrunk down to about eighteen male students during the last year. The equivalent grade of the girls' high school consisted of only five young ladies. We became an integrated class, the only one in our entire school, with surprising changes.

Before integration, the class atmosphere had often been one of rowdiness and silliness, with jokes, laughter, and often lack of attention to the teacher. With the girls present, the clowning totally stopped. All the guys sat in their seats, well behaved, paying close attention to the goings on up front. Nobody wanted to look stupid or silly in front of the women.

We had two new male students. Both were refugees from East Germany, which at that time was under Russian occupation. One was Klaus Rassmann. He had lost both of his parents in the East and was now living with a Protestant pastor's family in Solingen. He was an average student in class, but an outstanding pianist. He sometimes played for us on the grand piano in the auditorium of our school. He only played classical music.

One thing was peculiar about him, though. Klaus's pants had no buttons. Pants for boys or men normally had a row of buttons in front to keep the "fly" closed. Zippers were not popular yet. Instead of buttons, a stiff copper wire had been threaded through the buttonholes to keep the opening closed. It seemed that those were the only pair of pants he owned. We wondered how he was able to function that way but did not want to ask him.

CHAPTER THIRTY-ONE

THE GENIUS

The other new boy's name was Werner Kutzelnigg. I resented the fact we shared the same name. We just called him Kutzelnigg. He was different from all the other guys in class. In fact, he was totally different from anybody I had ever known. Kutzelnigg had a totally flat affect. One just could not connect with him. He usually just stood by himself, quietly smiling.

In sports, he seemed totally absent. Sometimes our sports teacher, Mr. Schuerner, would make us throw at each other and catch a large heavy ball, a medicine ball, about two feet in diameter. When the ball was thrown at Kutzelnigg, he would just stand and smile, and let the ball bounce off his chest. He would not even raise his arms or react in any way.

Our class went on a two-day bus excursion to the Mosel River with our English teacher, Miss Arlt. We hiked through vineyards, around ancient volcanic crater lakes in the Eiffel Mountains, and stayed overnight at a youth hostel. We slept in a large dormitory.

We decided to play a joke on Kutzelnigg, just to get his attention. At bedtime, with most everybody asleep, three of us sneaked over to his bed. He was lying on his back, sound asleep. We had a small can of black shoe polish with us. We painted his entire face carefully with the shoe polish. Surprisingly, he did not wake up. The next morning, we waited and watched. When he went to the common large bathroom, we saw him looking in the mirror, staring at his black face. There was no reaction, no outcry, nothing. He took a towel, soap and water, and slowly and laboriously worked the black polish off his face. He did not utter a single word to anybody.

On the way home to Solingen, the bus stopped at a restaurant for lunch. We had some extra time after eating and discovered a small bowling alley attached to the building. We all bowled, alternating. Kutzelnigg's turn came up. He picked up the ball, lifted it up to the side of his neck, then shot putted the ball upwards towards, and into, the ceiling. The ball disappeared in the ceiling through the large hole it created, pieces of sheetrock raining down on us.

We looked at Kutzelnigg, and we looked at each other, in disbelief. He showed no reaction. He just stood and smiled. We figured it was time to leave. We piled into the bus and left the scene. Kutzelnigg never uttered a single word about the incident.

Kutzelnigg was outstanding in one single field: mathematics.

By that time our class had progressed to trigonometry. I was totally lost, and so were most of my classmates. None of the teachers in our school could teach that subject. Once a week, a Professor of Mathematics from the University of Cologne traveled to Solingen to teach us. There was one time when the professor was writing numbers and formulas on the blackboard. We were all sitting there, staring. I don't think any of us understood what he was doing.

Kutzelnigg's hand went up. "I know an easier way," he said to the professor.

"You do? Please show me," said the professor.

Kutzelnigg walked to the blackboard and started writing numbers and equations. The professor watched in astonishment. He then said, "You are correct. That is an easier way. I never thought about it that way!" We had no idea what Kutzelnigg had written, but suddenly, he was our hero.

It was many years, perhaps 20 years later, when I attended a class reunion in Solingen. Kutzelnigg was there, looking happy and relaxed. I asked him, "How are you, and what have you done with your life?"

"I am professor of theoretical chemistry at Ruhr University Bochum," he replied with a self-assured smile.

It was years later, after I had studied medicine and psychology in California, that I became aware of a mental or psychological state called Asperger's syndrome. The person thus affected displays very low social skills, but exceeds immensely in one area of science, often mathematics, including abstract mathematics. I realized, then, that Kutzelnigg had Asperger's Syndrome. Albert Einstein, known worldwide as a genius in mathematics and related science, also had Asperger's syndrome.

CHAPTER THIRTY-TWO

VACATION IN BAVARIA

It was 1948, and we had undergone currency reform. It meant that one's bank accounts were worth ten percent of their original values. Older peoples' life savings were reduced to ten percent of their previous value. But the miracle was that overnight the grocery stores were full of the foods that, the day before, had only been available on the black market, and at exorbitant prices. One could buy something again with money.

Uncle Willi and Father decided to award Cousin Gert and I with a special present for the hardships we had endured the last few years. A two-week vacation in Bavaria! We were booked at a hotel in Traunstein, a town at the foot of the Alps. A customer of my father's company, who lived in the town, had volunteered to take us on a hike in the high Alps.

Gert and I traveled to Traunstein by train. It looked like a small, sleepy old town. We found the store of our parents' customer. We were shocked. It was what you could describe as a dry goods store, dimly lit chaos inside. We found our way to the back of the store, where our host welcomed us with a big smile and a hearty handshake.

"Gruess Gott!" (Greet God) he said. He was a rather small, unassuming man in his sixties, with a pleasant personality and a thick Bavarian accent.

"Gruess Gott," we answered.

After he showed us around in the store, proudly pointing out some Solingen knives made in our parents' factory, he started talking about the trip into the mountains he had planned for us. We would travel by bus to the foot of the Alps, and then start our ascent on a hiking trail. We would stay overnight at an Alm, halfway up the mountain. The following morning, we would continue up the mountain to the summit. Gross Gern was the name of the mountain. We would leave in two days, he said, and he would close his store during that time.

We needed to wear heavy mountain boots, which he said we could rent at our hotel. I asked about the shoes at the hotel. They did not have my size, and I had to settle for a larger size, to use with an extra pair of socks.

For reasons which escape me now, I had brought along from home my 24 bass accordion to play on the mountain. We met at the store in the early morning and got on the bus to the mountain. Each of us carried a small backpack, and I also carried my accordion. It was a slow walk up a narrow winding path, always upward. Our guide warned us to hike slowly, to not tire ourselves too much.

The weather was fine, and gradually beautiful views began to open up. It was midafternoon when we reached an area with broad, sloping green meadows. We had reached the Alm, our destination. There were a few brown and white cows scattered about, grazing. We could hear the clang clang of the large bells dangling from their necks, as they were slowly moving along. On one side of the meadow, we spotted several small, one-story buildings. Heavy rocks or boulders had been placed on their roofs, to secure them from heavy winds. As we approached, a man emerged from one of the buildings.

Our guide called out to him. They obviously knew each other. They greeted each other with big handshakes, and Cousin Gert and I were introduced. The two men spoke a language which was totally foreign to Gert and me. Our guide then translated. We asked him about the language. "That's the language the mountain people here speak!"

Our guide explained to us the operation of an alm in the mountains. In the spring, after the snow melted and the trails were open, the cows from the village were led up the mountain, to the alpine meadows. Around the neck of each cow a large bell was fastened. As the animal moved, the bell clanged, letting the herder know where each animal was located. In late afternoon, the herder milked the cows, and the milk was then carried down to the village by men from the village, walking up to the alms just for that purpose. This was a daily routine, lasting through the summer months.

In the fall the cows were led back down the trails to the village, all decorated, with a brass band playing, and the entire village celebrated the return of the cows for the approaching winter. The alpine milk was highly prized for its flavor, derived from the many mountain herbs and plants growing at altitude. Cheeses were made, also reflecting their alpine origin.

We slept in the hay of the barn, had a hearty breakfast of coffee with bread and cheese, packed our things, thanked the herder for his hospitality, and got on our way by mid-morning. I was carrying the accordion on my back, looking forward to playing some songs, in total solitude, on top of the magnificent mountain.

After an hour or so we were getting closer to the summit. I thought suddenly that I was hearing music coming from above. Brass band music? Was I hearing right? As we kept walking higher and higher, the sound of the music became louder. Then we began to hear human voices and laughter. I looked at our guide. He shrugged his shoulders.

"I believe there is a festival on the mountain," he said, "once a year."

As we got to the summit, the mountain top flattened out, and there in front of us were large numbers of people, all in Bavarian costumes, chatting, laughing, drinking beer, and having a wonderful time. There was music, a complete brass band with big tubas.

"But we did not see anybody coming up the mountain path behind us," I said. "How did they get the big tubas up here?"

"Oh," said our guide, "there is a back way up the mountain which is wide and easy. We will be going back down that way!"

It was a beautiful sight, all those happy people in costumes, and a big brass band playing. But I had brought my accordion all the way from Solingen to play in solitude on a mountain top. After enjoying the scenery, I sneaked off to get as far away as possible from the crowd and the music. I found an area with beautiful views. No people and no music. I sat down, shouldered my accordion, and played several songs at the meadows and mountains around me, as loud as I could. I felt a lot better.

I returned to the crowd. We spent a few hours walking around, enjoying the scenery and the happy atmosphere there. We ate the lunch we had brought up. Early in the afternoon, the band packed up their instruments and people began to leave. We followed them down the mountain, but this time on a broad gravel road.

That road became torture for me. My mountain boots were too large, and I found myself slipping and sliding forward in them. Slowly, it became painful for me to walk, and by the time we reached the valley floor, I was in great pain. I took off my boots after we got back to the hotel and found myself looking at a number of variably sized blisters on both my feet. It had been a great day, with a not-so-pleasant ending.

The following day things felt better. We joined our guide and host for dinner that evening. After a few beers he told us a story about himself.

CHAPTER THIRTY-THREE

MAKE ME A BUBERL!

When our guide was a young man, about twenty or so, he accidentally met a young woman about his age. They lived in the same small town but did not know each other.

They talked for a while. Then the girl suddenly invited him to visit her. Not for a normal social visit, but for a visit not uncommon in Bavaria, known as fensterln. Fenster is the German name for window. When a guy is invited to come fensterln, he comes in through the girl's bedroom window, in the middle of the night, to spend the night with her.

So, he was invited to spend the night with a girl he really did not know. She walked him over to her house and pointed out her bedroom window. It was on the second floor. She told him that the best time was after midnight, when her parents would be asleep.

He secured a ladder and waited until after midnight. He then walked over to her house, located her upstairs window and carefully placed the ladder under the window. It was about three feet short. While he was wondering what to do, the window above him opened. The girl appeared and motioned to him to climb up the ladder. When he had reached a rung close to the top of the ladder, he was too low to reach the windowsill.

As he was wondering what to do, the girl's alabaster white arm reached down to him. She grabbed him by the arm, and with one swift pull he was lifted and through the window. When they were in bed, she kept saying to him, "Make me a buberl, make me a buberl!"

Buberl is the word for baby boy in the Bavarian dialect. He left before dawn, sneaking down the stairs inside the house. She quietly closed the door behind him.

He walked over to the side of the house, got his ladder and went home, ladder over his shoulder. He never saw her again and had no idea whether he had made a baby, boy or girl.

Gert and I had two more days in Bavaria. It was a Saturday night. Our hotel had a ballroom, and we saw signs on the doors in the afternoon: Dance tonight! We thought it might be nice to go to a dance, although my feet were still hurting. We went downstairs in the evening, when we heard band music drifting up. We found a table for ourselves. The place was half filled with young people our age. We noticed that the tables were occupied by either girls or boys, but generally not mixed. That made it easier for us to get to dance with a girl, we thought.

A dance band was present, off to the side. We got up and walked over to a girls' table, to ask for a dance. Almost immediately, several young guys at neighboring tables got up and blocked us. "These are our girls," they said. "You are not dancing with them!"

They looked serious and threatening.

We stood there for a while, staring back at them. "Let's go," Gert said to me. "No use getting into a fight." We finished our beers and left. We walked up to our room, spontaneously singing our Solingen Heimat Song, a song praising the natural beauty of our hometown and its surroundings. We felt better after that.

We had two more days before we had to catch our train home. We stopped at a cheese shop selling local products. I bought a soft cheese, nicely packed in silver foil. Back at the hotel I opened the foil. I was going to make a sandwich. As I opened the foil, I noticed that the cheese was beginning to move. To my horror, I realized that I was looking at a mass of tightly packed maggots, which had replaced the cheese.

I closed the wrapping the best I could and ran back to the store.

I excitedly explained to the lady behind the counter that I had bought maggots instead of cheese. She opened the wrapper and looked inside. I expected her to toss the whole thing into the garbage can. But, to my complete surprise, she nonchalantly closed the wrapper and placed the entire package into the refrigerator behind her.

"It will be alright in a few days," she said. "You want a different cheese?" I bought a hard cheese instead. Back in Solingen we had quite a story to tell.

CHAPTER THIRTY-FOUR

JOINING THE BAND

I had started piano lessons again, but I did not go back to my first teacher, Frau Wietscher. Once a year Frau Wietscher gave a concert with her students, for parents and friends. Frau Wietscher also sang solo soprano on stage on those occasions. Father was not impressed. "She sings like a chicken in heat," he always said. I figured he knew, since we had chickens at home.

Mr. Kronenberg became my new teacher. He was a gentle man with a mild disposition, and long artist's hair down to his shoulders. When I made a mistake by hitting a wrong key, he did not make me start all over again, as my previous teacher had done. I was playing classical music only, and practicing one hour every day, after school. Mother always made sure of that.

Mr. Kronenberg told me that he had worked for several years on composing an Opera based on Grimm's fairy tale Hansel and Gretel. He had finished it and had kept the script in his house. During an air raid on Solingen, his house burned down. His work was gone.

One day, a young man appeared at our house. He was looking for a piano player. He told me he had been sent by a friend who had a small dance band. I told him that I only played classical music. He suggested that I perhaps go to one of the weekly rehearsals and talk with the members there.

I was curious and decided to go. The rehearsal was held in the backroom of a local pub, on a Thursday night. There I met KarlAugust Arzt, accordion player and director. Armin played bass, and Kuhner played electric guitar. They seemed like nice guys, all in their early twenties. They explained to me that they were all amateur musicians with other daytime jobs. They enjoyed playing at small events like birthday parties, weddings, and holiday events. They had lost their piano player and were looking for a new one. I sat in on the rehearsal and took some sheet music home for practice.

The following week, I was back and started to play with them. I liked it and found it more interesting than playing just classical music by myself. Pretty soon I got into the swing of things and started to really enjoy playing, especially when realizing that the audience appreciated our music. And I got paid real money after an engagement. I did not have to ask my father for pocket money anymore.

Word apparently got around about us. We started having regular Friday and Saturday night engagements at different places, such as the Wasserturm restaurant, restaurants in Old Graefrath, and Cafe Muller. The Cafe was special for me, since it was a small intimate place, frequented by actors and singers from the Solingen Opera. We sometimes found ourselves accompanying professional singers. I still remember, with some pain, an actress telling me that technically I was very good, but that I had not yet developed the sensitivity of expression that some songs required.

It was early 1951. KarlAugust told us one day he had been contacted by the owner of a bar and restaurant in Solingen Wald, with a large indoor dance floor and a large outdoor public swimming pool. The owner was looking for a full time (Friday evenings, Saturday and Sunday afternoons and evenings) dance band. Were we interested? We talked it over. It sounded very interesting and challenging. And the money was very good. We got paid by the hour. We agreed to apply for the job. However, in order to get the contract for one year we had to compete with three other bands, also applying for the job.

On a Sunday afternoon we were there to compete. The three other bands preceded us. We thought they were all OK. Then came our turn.

We played two songs. We did fine, we thought. The audience was invited to cast ballots. We won. The contract was ours!

The restaurant owner asked us whether we could perhaps add a member to our band, a drummer, who had played with the previous band, but who was out of a job now. We were so happy to have won the competition, we said, "yes", after we met and talked with him. His name was Bobby.

The following weekend we started. There was a large dance floor, and it was usually packed. Bobby fitted in well and we liked him. He told us that he was a refugee from East Germany. He had come West with his father, escaping the Russian occupation.

We had a very appreciative audience, flooding us with drinks. Every evening the top of my upright piano was totally covered with various drinks, from beer to vodka, wine and liqueurs. We could not possibly consume all those presents, or we would have passed out. Bobby worked out the problem. After closing for the evening, he produced an empty liter bottle or two into which he poured all the strong drinks, no matter what type. "For my father," he told us. Truly mixed drinks. We did not even dare to guess what that wild mixture tasted like.

Between attending high school, and playing piano on weekends, I was very busy. I did not have time to spend with my other friends anymore. I was having so much fun, and it started to take its toll on my grades in school. I was barely hanging on to my grade in mathematics. My teacher advised me to perhaps take private math lessons from Kutzelnigg, my brilliant classmate. I got together with him a few times, but it did not help.

Sometimes while playing in the band, I had the math book propped up on the piano, where the sheet music should have been, trying to study. I was just kidding myself. My final grade was a D.

CHAPTER THIRTY-FIVE

PARIS, PARIS!

It was early July 1951. Mr. Brendel, our French teacher and war hero who shot off Russian tanks, had a surprise announcement.

During the August summer vacation, the entire class would be going to Paris, France, and tour adjacent areas in France, for a total of three weeks. We were speechless. What a great idea, what a great surprise! It would be our last summer together, since the following year was graduation.

I told the exciting news to my musician friends. KarlAugust, our band leader, was a little concerned, since our contract with the bar/restaurant lasted through the end of the year. I went to the bar owner/manager and told him that I would be gone for four weeks in August, since my entire high school class was going to Paris. He was not too happy, since I did not have a replacement piano player. I told him I had no choice but to go with my class. He finally said, "Well, if you have to go with your school, then it has to be that way." He told me that he had been stationed in Paris while in the German army, and that he really liked the city. He asked me to send him a postcard while there, and to tell him about my experiences after I got back. I happily agreed.

Class always ended on the top of the hour, when a loud bell rang throughout the building, announcing the end of classes. The teacher would end his/her lecture, maybe make a few comments about the next session, and then leave. We would have ten minutes until the next teacher entered, to start his/her lesson. We would have just enough time to run to the bathroom, if needed.

Mr. Brendel, our French teacher, had one bad habit. For some reason not clear to us, he was not bothered by the end-of-class bell. He would go on talking and lecturing, and quite often our next teacher would be entering our classroom while Brendel was still teaching. We did not quite know how to break Brendel of this habit.

I had an idea. We would put an alarm clock in Mr. Brendel's desk, up front by the blackboard, to go off at the top of the hour. Everybody thought it was a great idea. Klaus Rassmann, the boy with the wired fly in his pants, volunteered to bring his bedside alarm clock. The following day he brought the clock, with two old-fashioned bells on top.

Before Brendel came to class, I wound up the clock, set the alarm to the top of the hour, and placed it in Brendel's desk up front by the blackboard. The hour went by with Brendel talking. The school bell rang in the hallway. Brendel kept talking, and the alarm clock went off with a rather loud sound. Brendel stopped, looked around, and walked towards the students, until he realized that the sound was somewhere behind him. He walked back to his desk and opened it. He was looking at the alarm clock, which was happily sounding off at him.

His face turned red with fury. "Whose clock is this?" he shouted.

Rassmann stood up. "It's mine," he said quietly.

Brendel turned on Rassmann. But before he could lay into him, I stood up and said loudly, "Mr. Brendel, I put the clock into your desk. I borrowed it from Rassmann."

Brendel turned towards me. "Get that clock out of my desk, NOW!" I walked over to the desk and removed the clock, while the whole class was watching in silence.

"Stamm," Brendel said, "I will talk with you after class!" After everybody had left, I waited for Brendel. "You are NOT going to Paris with the rest of the class. I am canceling you out. Dismissed!"

I did not feel that there was any point in arguing with him. I turned and left. I had really been looking forward to that trip. So, that was it.

I was not allowed to go. What to do now? I had already told the owner of the bar and restaurant that I would be going to Paris for four weeks.

CHAPTER THIRTY-SIX

HEADING SOUTH, LAKE CHIEMSEE

I talked to my classmate and friend Micki. He said that he was not really interested in going to Paris with the class. He would rather do something else. After some back and forth, we planned to get on our bicycles and head for the Bavarian Alps, more specifically Mount Watzmann near Berchtesgaden. I confided in one of my classmates where I was going and asked him to do me a big favor. When in Paris, would he please send a postcard from there to the restaurant in Ittertal where we played, and sign my name to it? He promised to do that.

After school was out for the summer, Micki and I started packing for our trip. Since we could not use the Autobahn with our bikes, we took the scenic route up the Rhine River, to Heidelberg, the ancient University town, past the Black Forest and Munich, and toward beautiful Lake Chiemsee at the foot of the Alps.

We got to the lake after five days. The weather was beautiful. The lake was beautiful. We decided to stay overnight in the little sleepy town of Chieming, directly on the lake. We found a farmhouse, where the farmer let us sleep in the hay barn for almost no money.

The following day, we decided to go swimming in the lake. The water was great, crystal clear and not too cold. As we got away from the shore, we spotted a floating wooden platform anchored to the lake bottom, inviting swimmers to rest.

We climbed up from the water and saw a young woman resting there, sunbathing. We said "Hello," and sat down. She seemed a little older than us. She was very good looking. After a few minutes, we started a conversation. We told her where we were from, that we were traveling on our bicycles, and after leaving the lake we were going to climb the Watzmann mountain by Berchtesgaden. She told us that she was on vacation from a small town not far away, Altotting, and that she had come by train.

After a while we all went for a swim, then got out of the water and sat on the sandy beach together. Ursula was her name, she told us. She took a picture of Micki and I sitting on the sand, with my camera. We wanted to take a picture of her also, but she declined. Dinner time came. She knew a little rustic restaurant nearby.

We got a table inside. I was seated next to Ursula, Micki across from us. We started with a tall beer or two. My right hand was around the beer mug, my left hand rested on my thigh. After a while I felt her hand coming over to my leg, then pulling my hand over and onto her thigh and holding it there. I felt almost paralyzed and did not quite know what to do. But I enjoyed the feeling of her smooth warm skin.

After dinner, we walked back into the village. We stopped at a nice-looking large farmhouse. She was renting a room there, she told us. Our barn was a short walk from there. We had to get up early the next morning to get to Berchtesgaden and the mountain. We said goodbye. She wished us a fun trip.

CHAPTER THIRTY-SEVEN

THE WATZMANN EXPERIENCE

It took us over two hours to get to Berchtesgaden. That picturesque little town lies on the shore of the Konigsee, a spectacular lake from which the Watzmann mountain rises majestically.

We stored our bikes at the railroad station and started walking up the mountain hiking trail, carrying only small backpacks with food, water and our cameras. Small groups of hikers were above, as well as below us. The upward hike would take several hours. At about eleven o'clock we decided to stop for a break right by the trail. We sat on large boulders, enjoying a sandwich and some water we had brought along. We then continued up, walking slowly. The views became increasingly more beautiful.

At one point we stopped. It was time to take a picture. I got out my camera. Micki was looking through his bag for his camera. He could not find it. He searched again. No camera! He turned ashen white.

"That's my mother's camera," he said, "I borrowed it from her just for this trip. I must have left it where we took the sandwich break."

We raced down the trail, passing hikers coming up and going down. We got to the rocks where we had sat. Nothing there. We looked and searched everywhere, behind the rocks, underneath the rocks. Nothing. Did somebody find the camera and take it?

Micki thought for a while, then said, "I have to go back to Solingen right now. That camera was expensive, and I have to get a job to make money to buy my mother a new one."

I suggested, "Could we perhaps go up to the top of the mountain, I would take some pictures, and then we would hurry back down to town?"

"No," he said. "I must take the next train to Munich and from there to Solingen. Are you coming with me?"

A thought flared up in my mind. "I am going back down to Berchtesgaden with you, but I am not taking the train to Munich. I am staying here a while longer." I knew where I was going. I was going to head back to Lake Chiemsee!

After we got back down from the mountain, Micki bought his train ticket for the afternoon train to Munich. We said goodbye. I got on my bike and started pedaling. I had quite a distance to go.

I got back to Chieming in the early evening. I was quite tired. I stopped at the farmhouse where I had slept before and laid down in the hay.

CHAPTER THIRTY-EIGHT

HAPPY BIRTHDAY!

I felt refreshed when I woke up the next morning. It was August 26, my birthday. I was twenty years old! I wondered what the day would be like. Certainly not the traditional birthday party with my friends in Solingen. I was anxious to see Ursula.

It was about eight o'clock. I got up, dusted off my clothes, and walked over to the farmhouse where Ursula was staying. The double door to the ground floor stood wide open. I stepped inside. There she was, standing in the large foyer, holding a cup of coffee on a saucer. She turned towards me. As she recognized me, her coffee cup started dancing and rattling on the saucer.

She was speechless for a moment. "You came back?" she breathed.

"Yes, I was hoping to see you again," I said. I told her the story about Micki losing his camera on the mountain.

Ursula was beaming. "I am so happy you came back!" She took me upstairs to show me her room. It was spacious, with a table and chairs, a couch, a bed and a bathroom. We had breakfast together, then went outside to walk into town and down to the beach.

The day somehow went by in a hurry. Evening came. I had told Ursula that it was my birthday. She picked a nice restaurant she knew and invited me to dinner. We had a great meal of lake fish with a bottle of white wine.

She asked me where I had slept the night before. I told her, and she said, "You are staying with me tonight!"

Staying with a woman overnight? For the first time in my life, and on my birthday, spending a night with a woman? I wondered later, was it destiny, or whatever you want to call it, that Micki had to lose his camera on the mountain?

We spent the following four days together, inseparable and happy. Then came Sunday, when she had to go back home. She had to start work again on Monday. We walked to the train station together. The train was on time. We hugged for a long time and said goodbye.

I was so anxious to see Uschi, as I called her, again soon, if possible.

CHAPTER THIRTY-NINE

HOMEBOUND DISASTER

The following morning, I packed my things, loaded them on the bike, and set out for Munich. I could not use the Autobahn and had to travel on country roads.

I had been told about a huge parking lot for overnight parking for long distance trucks, on the outskirts of Munich. I did not savor a four-day trip by bicycle back to Solingen and thought I might perhaps hitch a ride back close to home on the back of a truck headed that way.

I got to Munich by midafternoon and was lucky to find the truck parking lot, next to the Autobahn. I lazily cruised around among at least a hundred trucks parked there, looking at the signs on the doors of the cabs, each listing their home ports. There was a truck from Dusseldorf, which is an about one hour's bike ride from Solingen!

It had a big flat bed, loaded with something, covered with a tarp. But there was nobody to ask. I waited for several hours, when two men showed up and got into the cab. I walked over and introduced myself, saying I was from Solingen, and would they allow me to catch a ride on the back of their truck to Dusseldorf? They looked at me, sizing me up, I thought, and talked among themselves. They said it was OK.

They were leaving at 6:00 AM in the morning. They suggested that I load all my things, including my bike, on the truck bed now, and to be back at six. I could not sleep on the truck bed however, they stated.

I was so happy to have found a ride. I loaded my things on the back of the truck, including my bike, trusting it would be OK to leave them there.

Where would I sleep? I walked around, looking. I spotted an old long abandoned American Army jeep sitting forlorn all by itself. I climbed in and settled in one of the two seats. I dozed off a few times, waking up, checking my watch. I could not miss my ride to Dusseldorf at 6 AM.

I was awakened by a truck engine which had started up somewhere not far away. I checked my watch. It was 5 AM. The truck was moving away slowly. I raised my head to see. I looked again. Could it be? It looked like my truck. But I could only see a silhouette in the dim light. I climbed out of the jeep and ran over towards the truck which was moving away and gaining speed.

It was my truck! I ran, shouting, but it was pulling away from me. I could not catch up with it. Just to be sure, I ran over to where my truck had been parked. The spot was empty. My truck was gone, with all my belongings! I did not know whether I should scream in anger or cry.

I stood there for a while, feeling lost. After walking around for a long time, I spotted another parked truck with the name Dusseldorf on the door. I waited for an hour or two, when the driver walked up. I told him my story and asked whether he was driving to Dusseldorf. He nodded, "Yes." I then told him the name of the trucking company which had left me behind. He said he knew those people, and where in Dusseldorf they were located.

"Could you give me a ride?" I asked.

I could ride on the load area in the back, he said. But he would drive to his own location in Dusseldorf only. I gladly accepted. By midmorning we took off. The truck carried a load of tar paper rolls, standing up on end. I sat on the tar paper, not caring about the round imprints on my pants. By afternoon we arrived in Dusseldorf. The driver stopped at one point in the city and told me how to get to the company I was looking for. I thanked him greatly for his kindness and started walking.

I don't remember how long it took me to find the trucking company, but I was extremely relieved to finally see my truck parked in an open yard, in front of a home. It was still loaded, but my bike and my other belongings were not on the truck. I walked deeper into the yard and spotted my bicycle leaning against the wall of the house. I then saw the truck driver coming out of the house. He was not too happy to see me.

I confronted him, saying that he left Munich without me, taking all my belongings with him. He was half apologetic. I pointed to my bicycle leaning against the wall. A woman came out from the house asking what was going on. I told her that all my clothes and other belongings had been on the truck also. She denied knowing anything or having any of those things in her possession. Her husband took her aside, whispering to her. She then went into the house and came out carrying my bags which had been on the truck.

"Here is your stuff," she said in a gruff voice, and walked back into the house. I loaded up my bicycle, walked it out of the yard, and got on my way.

About two hours later I arrived home in Solingen. I had quite a story to tell, and also not to tell. The following weekend I was back playing dance music with our band. The restaurant owner asked me how I liked Paris.

I loved it there, I told him.

CHAPTER FORTY

CALL FROM THE EMBASSY

I received a letter from the American Embassy in Hamburg in October 1951. I was scheduled for a personal interview and physical examination regarding my application for immigration to the United States, for November 1951. The process had started about two and a half years prior.

Fred Graebe, a former classmate of mine at the Humboldt School, had immigrated together with his parents to the United States about three years before. Fred's father, a structural engineer, had been a witness against the Nazis at the Nuremberg Trial. He was the only German who had testified as an eyewitness to the atrocities and mass killings the Nazis had committed during World War II against the Jews, in the then German-occupied Ukraine.

After the trial, Mr. Graebe received death threats from ex-Nazis in Germany. Fearing for his and his family's safety, and with the help of a U.S.-based Jewish organization, he was able to immigrate to the United States, with his wife and son.

(NOTE: The details of Mr. Graebe's accounts, chronicling his experiences as a civil engineer in the Ukraine during World War II, and as an eyewitness to the Nazi atrocities, are documented in the book *The Moses of Rovno*, by Douglas K. Huneke, published in the US. Copyright 1985, Compassion House)

After the family's resettlement in San Francisco, California, I kept in touch with Fred, the son. I had told him that I wanted to study medicine, but there was a two-year waiting period at the universities in Germany, in order to first accommodate applicant ex-medics from the WWII German Armed Forces.

Fred wrote back, saying that he had talked to his parents about me, and that they offered to sponsor me to immigrate to the US, so that I could study medicine there without a waiting period.

I was totally excited about this offer. I told my parents who also seemed in favor of my chance to study medicine abroad. My only other option at that time seemed to be an office job at Bayer chemical company near Dusseldorf. I had inquired there and was given a tour of the plant and offices. The office complex looked like a small town, consisting of a number of lookalike buildings with multiple doors arranged in a linear fashion. I would be working in one of those offices. My impression was totally negative and raised no enthusiasm in me, to say the least.

The offer from the Graebes in San Francisco sounded like an exciting alternative, a once-in-a-lifetime chance, which I could not turn down. I applied to US Immigration. It was now two and a half years later that I received a letter to come for an interview by US Immigration at the US Embassy in Hamburg.

I went to Hamburg by train. The interview at the American Embassy went well, I thought. I also had a physical examination with a chest x-ray. I passed but was told that my chest film showed a small, calcified nodule in the middle of my chest, probably relating back to my childhood, possibly representing a spot of healed tuberculosis.

CHAPTER FORTY-ONE

GHOST IN THE CLOSET

On the way home on the train, I started thinking. Tuberculosis? It was something I had never even thought about in relation to me. I had been in and out of doctors' offices many times during my childhood, for various things including rickets, but I had never had a chest x-ray. However, I had heard about tuberculosis a few times.

Father told me once that both his oldest sister and brother had died of the disease in their twenties. I also remembered a time when Father and I were in the railroad station restaurant in Solingen Wald. I had to go to the men's room. A man was standing there, coughing violently, when suddenly a large amount of blood gushed from his mouth, and he collapsed on the floor. I ran out, scared, telling my father. He talked to the restaurant owner, and a short while later an ambulance arrived. "Probably open tuberculosis," Father said.

And on a beautiful Sunday morning my friend Gert, another friend by the name of Hans, and I went on a hike through the forest to the Wupper river, about a mile away. On the way back, Hans started to cough. He stopped, and while coughing, a large amount of bright red blood issued from his mouth. He turned white and sat down. The city hospital was about a mile away. We had to get him to the hospital. We pulled him up, steadied him by supporting him by his shoulders, and walked him to the hospital as fast as we could. He was admitted immediately.

We never saw him again, but heard that the diagnosis was tuberculosis, and that he had been transferred to a tuberculosis sanitarium outside the city.

A few years prior, after the war had ended, I had met a lady tailor whose teenage daughter had also been admitted to a tuberculosis sanitarium. My mother had taken me to the lady to have an overcoat made for me for the approaching winter. Since one could not buy any clothing in stores, Mother had brought with us a blanket from my bed. I was measured, and a week or so later the blanket coat was ready. To my horror, the lady had fashioned a beautiful lady's coat for me. It buttoned from right to left, but the worst thing was that it flared out beautifully from the waist down. It looked really good on my mother. The lady apologized; she was not used to making men's clothing.

We had no material for her to start over again. Winter came, and I had to wear the coat. I was so embarrassed that somebody might look at me, that I did not button the coat but let it hang down loosely and open in the front, even in the bitter cold. To my surprise, nobody seemed to notice, not even the beautifully raised edges of the shoulders.

CHAPTER FORTY-TWO

ACCEPTED FOR IMMIGRATION

About three weeks later a letter arrived from the American Embassy in Hamburg. I was afraid to open it.

It said YOU HAVE BEEN ACCEPTED FOR IMMIGRATION TO THE UNITED STATES OF AMERICA! I raced around, showing my letter to everybody. I could not believe it was real. But it was! My parents were elated, it seemed. But Mother said, "Do you really want to go?"

"Yes, I do," I shouted.

The letter said that I had 6 months to leave for the US, which was the end of April 1952. If I failed to do so, I would have to apply all over again. But my high school graduation was in June! And our dance band contract would still be in force. I had also planned on seeing Uschi again, over New Years in Frankfurt, but that could work out OK.

I talked to my cousin Heinz, who had also applied for immigration. He had received the same notice as I. We would leave together. The embassy also told us that the *SS America* would be sailing from the seaport of Bremerhafen, Germany, on March 20, 1952, and that reservations should be made. I had to get busy.

So many things to think of and to do. I wrote a letter to Uschi in Bavaria, telling her about my departure in March. She never answered me. Perhaps no love lost. I went to the principal of my high school and gave him the news. How could I graduate before the end of the school year? He said, "Congratulations!" and he would work on it.

My friends in the dance band were excited for me, but also sad to see me leave.

I notified my sponsors, the Graebe family in San Francisco, of my coming. They sounded equally excited. I was told also that the German Mark currency was not convertible into US dollars yet, and that my passage would have to be paid in dollars. So, I had to turn to my sponsors for that. The Greabe family graciously would pay for my entire trip in advance, by ship to New York, and by train from New York to Oakland, California, and that they would find a job for me in San Francisco so that I could pay them back later. Everything seemed to fall into place.

I wrote to my two pen pal friends in the US, Virginia Schoonover in Denver, Colorado, and Maxine Venable in Hayward, California. They wrote back to me. Both were anxious to meet me. Time seemed to fly suddenly. Christmas and New Year's came and went. My High School principal told me that he had contacted the school authorities at the state level in Duesseldorf. A delegation of examiners from the School Board in Duesseldorf would travel to Solingen to give me a special final examination at my school.

CHAPTER FORTY-THREE

FINAL EXAMINATION

The delegation of examiners from the state capital of Duesseldorf had arrived. I was told that the examination would be verbal and would take about three hours. I was sweating blood. I did not know what to expect.

I was ushered into the room set aside for my trial. There were six stern-looking gentlemen I had never seen before, seated before me on a row of chairs. Behind them sat my teachers. They looked just as nervous as I was feeling, I thought.

After a few friendly introductory remarks, the session began. Everybody knew of course that I was immigrating to the US. I was asked about the American Constitution, a subject we had not covered in class. Then came questions about the history of the United States. I squeezed by, I felt. Then the examination about my knowledge of English, French and Latin. I did OK there, I felt. Then questions about European history. Mathematics, my worst feared subject, was no problem, since there was no blackboard. I worked my way through the answers, with some encouraging nods occasionally from one or two of my teachers. The whole session seemed like a nightmare, but it finally ended.

The head of the delegation stood up, thanked everybody for their efforts, and then I was asked to walk down the line of examiners, shaking hands with everybody, and thanking them for their good will wishes. I had successfully passed. I kept going to school until my date of departure, but I felt no pressure, a strange feeling, since I already had my grades.

In February, the entire school celebrated the annual Carnival Season with a big party in a restaurant. Since I played in a dance band, my high school principal asked me to suggest a suitable location for the event. And would our band be willing to play at the event? It sounded too good to be true.

I suggested the Ittertal Resort, with a large restaurant, dance floor, large, landscaped area with a pond and a Fairy Tale Forest in the hills behind the property. Our band got the contract for the music. The school would pay us!

It was a grand party. The only problem for me was that I could not dance, since I was part of the band.

CHAPTER FORTY-FOUR

GETTING READY FOR DEPARTURE

I was notified by the American Embassy that my date of departure from Germany was March 20, 1952. Passage for me had been booked on the *SS America*. The ship would leave from the port of Bremerhaven. Prior to that I had to go to the American Embassy in Hamburg to receive my final immigration and travel papers. I checked with my cousin Heinz. He had received identical instructions. We would be traveling together.

My parents, in the meantime, had developed very mixed feelings about my departure, especially Mother. She had feelings of joy, mixed with sadness and anger. I was her only child, and I was leaving, going to a place half a world away.

I was full of joy and anticipation, mixed with anxiety. I had no family where I was going, and a lot of uncertainty, aside from having a language problem and no financial support. I was facing a real adventure.

Mother had one last job for me. "Before you leave," she said, "you have to empty the septic tank and carry the sewage down into the garden. That will be fertilizer for the spring planting."

She was angry, I realized, but the die had been cast. It took me two days. I used a medium-sized bucket on a long handle to dip into the sewage in the septic tank. I then filled two larger buckets with the foul-smelling brown chunky material, brown liquid and strips of paper. I carried them down into our garden about 100 feet away, then dumped everything on the still partially frozen ground.

Packing my belongings was easy. I had one medium sized suitcase and one briefcase.

CHAPTER FORTY-FIVE

GOODBYE, SOLINGEN

It was March 18, 1952. We all gathered at the railroad station in Solingen Ohligs, waiting for the train to Hamburg. My parents, uncles and aunts, all my friends were there, and of course my cousin and travel companion Heinz. He said to me jokingly, "In a couple of days my name will be Henry." I had no way of converting my name so easily. In fact, I could not even pronounce my first name in English.

My musician friends had brought their instruments and played our favorite songs on the station platform while we were standing and talking. This was goodbye, for how long nobody knew. Heinz and I were traveling into the unknown.

The train approached the station. We looked at each other. This was it, the time to say goodbye had come. One last hug with family and friends, and Heinz and I climbed aboard. We waved and waved from the train, until the station was out of sight.

CHAPTER FORTY-SIX

HAMBURG

We got to Hamburg by late afternoon. Hamburg at that time was a city which lay mainly in ruins after the WW II bombings.

Heinz and I had been booked into a low-cost hotel for the night, the Bunker Hotel. And a bunker it was. It had the shape of a huge bomb standing on its tail. Most of Hamburg had been reduced to rubble during the war, but the bunker was still standing. It looked just like the one in Solingen, in which everybody had died.

We were shown to our room. The circular concrete staircase inside had been partitioned off into numerous very small box-like rooms peripherally, with a door connecting to the central walkway. A two-bed bunk was in our room. There was no running water, and no toilet. Those were located elsewhere in the building. There was a small rectangular hole in the thick concrete wall, the window. We managed to get our baggage into the room. To get undressed in the evening and go to bed, one of us had to step out into the hallway, waiting for the person inside to get into the bunk.

The next morning, we found our way to the American Embassy, where we got our Visas and traveling documents, and our tickets for our ship in Bremerhaven. We spent most of the day at the famous Hagenbeck Zoo, which had survived the war. And we visited the famous Elbe Tunnels, which descend deep under the Elbe River, allowing large steamships to pass overhead.

CHAPTER FORTY-SEVEN

GOODBYE, GOODBYE!

March 20, 1952. Heinz and I took the train to Bremerhaven. The port of Hamburg was not adequate for accommodating large passenger ships.

Our ship, the *USS United States*, was anchored at the port of Bremerhaven and scheduled to leave shortly after noon that day. Our train stopped not far from the pier. The ship was enormous. It looked like a giant mountain, when looking at it from the ground. After our papers were checked and the baggage was tagged with our cabin number, we walked up the gangway. We were handed information about the location of our cabin, mealtimes, and entertainment. Heinz and I had been assigned to the same cabin, several floors below the main deck.

We found our cabin, which held two bunk beds for a total of four passengers, and a small bathroom with a toilet. Two German guys, about our age, showed up. They had also been assigned to our cabin. I picked a lower bunk and stashed my belongings.

We went back up to the deck to watch the departure. Passengers were still arriving and coming on board. Baggage was being loaded. While standing and watching I felt a sudden urge to empty my bladder. I tried to ignore it for a while, but the pressure got stronger. I had to go, now!

I walked around, looking for a bathroom. Thank heavens, I found one. I lifted the lid on the toilet seat. I was looking at a bowl filled with water. Oh no, I said to myself, the toilet is plugged, or not working yet. I cannot flush it!

What to do? I raced downstairs to our cabin. I could not hold it any longer. I lifted the lid, and ... oh no! It was the same there. The bowl was full of water! At that point I did not care. I emptied my bladder into the bowl. What a relief! After that, I pushed the valve lever, not caring what was going to happen next. And to my amazement, the toilet just flushed! I could not believe it. This was very different. German flush toilets do not have water standing in the bowl, only just a little water in the very bottom.

Totally relieved and having learned a lesson, I walked back up to the deck, which was now packed with passengers, talking excitedly, pushing against the railing to catch a glimpse of the crowd on the pier below. The brass band was playing the traditional departure song, "*Muss I denn, Muss I denn, aus dem Staedele heraus...*"

The huge cables holding the ship in place were dropped into the water, a deep rumble started in the bowels of the ship, and one could feel the ship moving slowly. In order to get a somewhat better view of the goings-on, I had climbed up on a ledge next to one of the ship's huge chimney stacks. I had a good view from there. Suddenly, there were several short enormously loud, low-sounding blasts right above my head, accompanied by a fierce vibration of whatever I was standing on. It almost made me sink down to my knees. It took me a few seconds to realize that the blasts had come from the ship's huge horns, saying goodbye to everybody, and that we were underway.

Slowly, very slowly, the ship distanced itself from the port, accompanied by several small tugboats, looking like insects in the water surrounding the huge ship. I stood there, looking back.

Goodbye, goodbye, Germany. Goodbye, my parents, my family, my friends, my home.

I did not exactly know how I was feeling. Sad, excited and happy, worried about what I was facing. I was floating into a new world, into a big unknown.

CHAPTER FORTY-EIGHT

UNDERWAY

Slowly, ever so slowly, the land became more distant. People on the deck walked off in different directions, and the hum of the ship's engines became more prominent. The waters were calm, and the horizon presented as a steady straight line around the ship.

After a few hours, land was in sight again. We were looking at England. We moved closer. We were approaching a large city with a large port. "Southampton," came the announcement over the loudspeakers.

Slowly, the ship eased into a dock. After we had tied up, people started coming aboard. After about an hour or so, the cables holding our ship in place dropped into the water, and we were on our way again. A few hours later we were approaching land again. "Ireland," came the announcement over the loudspeaker. But there was no harbor. The ship's engines seemed to almost stop, then reverse, and we saw a small boat approaching. The boat came alongside. Cables were dropped from our ship, pulling the boat close and against our side. A door opened on our ship, way down close to the water line. We could see a gangplank coming out from our ship and connecting with the small boat. Passengers and baggage came aboard. After everything was disconnected and the small boat moved back towards land, our ship's engines came back to life, and we headed away from Ireland.

Heinz and I walked around the ship, trying to get acquainted with our surroundings. The upper decks with passenger cabins, restaurants and bars were apparently occupied by First Class passengers and were

OFF LIMITS to passengers like us. We could use the outside areas of the main lower deck but had to walk down gangways to get to the lower levels for the dining room, movie theater and other facilities. To get to our cabin, we had to go down several more sloping walkways with handrails on both sides.

Our dining room was large, with bullseyes on both sides showing the sky and numerous tables for four to six persons. The four of us from our cabin were assigned a table in the dining room. Mealtimes and other announcements came over loudspeakers in the hallways and dining room.

Our two roommates were from the Black Forest area and about our age. Just like us, neither of them had ever been on a ship before.

CHAPTER FORTY-NINE

STORMY WEATHER

The first few days on the ship were uneventful. The meals were alright, and there were movies in the evening. We were able to get an occasional beer from the bar upstairs, paying cash. I spent a lot of time during the day standing on the large deck outside, looking at the horizon, which gave me a feeling of stability with only mild movements of the ship under my feet.

But that did not last. Winds were increasing gradually, the waves were developing white caps, and the ship started to move in very unpleasant ways. The bow started going up and down, and, worst of all, the ship started tilting from right to left, and from left to right. Visiting the dining room to eat became a real challenge. When looking at the bullseye on your left you would see the sky, whereas on the right the bullseye was under water. A few seconds later it would be the reverse. Food on the table would start to move from right to left, from left to right, and up and down. An orange at breakfast would roll all over and often leave the table. To bend down to retrieve the orange would become a real challenge.

I had to force myself to stay seated at the table and to swallow my food. The face of one of my cabinmates was turning white. I looked at my cousin Heinz. He and the other Black Forest guy were eating and chatting as if everything was fine and in order.

After suffering through three or four meals, I decided to go to my cabin and lie down. I was not the only one in bad shape, I found out. On the way back to the cabin the hallway was slippery with vomit, and the stench became unbearable. I had to hang onto the railing along the walkway to avoid slipping and falling into the mess. When I got to the cabin, one of the Black Forest guys was right behind me. We climbed into our cots and laid down. After a while I felt much better, although the ship's movements had not diminished.

We developed a system which worked for the two of us for the duration of the storm, which lasted three more days. At mealtimes, we would call the cabin steward and ask for him to bring the food to the cabin. I would then eat my meal lying on my bed. After an hour or so I would get up and go to the deck upstairs where I would breathe fresh air and where I was able to fix my eyes on the horizon.

This went on for several days. Heinz and his Black Forest buddy were having a good time, whereas the other Black Forest guy and I spent our days mainly horizontally in our bunks, getting by that way.

The scheduled five-day trip to New York had now become an eight-day trip because of the storm.

CHAPTER FIFTY

NEW YORK, NEW YORK

Finally, the weather improved, and the seas calmed. I began to feel that I would make it, my stomach now settling down even when standing upright.

There was a gala evening with a special dinner and alcoholic drinks, on our last night before arriving in New York. The hallways had been cleaned of vomit and the ship looked fine. Over the speakers, the captain thanked us for traveling on the United States Line and apologized for the inclement weather and the delay in arrival. Tomorrow was March 28, 1952, and we would be arriving in New York Harbor by mid-morning. The day would be cool, with possible rain.

I slept well that last night in my bunk and laid out my clothes to wear the following day. After breakfast we placed our tagged baggage for pickup in the hallway outside our cabins. I went up to the deck after that to watch for land to come into sight. Slowly, ever so slowly, a gray line appeared at the horizon which appeared to be land. The ship was steady, the horizon was steady, and we were moving slowly closer and closer to our destination. We finally began to see outlines of tall buildings. New York! One could feel happy tensions rise in anticipation.

And there it came into view, the famous Statue of Liberty, thrusting her torch toward the sky. The ship's engines quieted down, and we began to slow down considerably, gliding along quietly towards our pier. The New York skyline moved closer and closer, and the buildings appeared to be growing in front of us.

We docked. There were final instructions over the loudspeakers about the disembarking process. People were lining up in long queues. Cousin Heinz and I stood together. He told me he was being picked up on the pier by people he had been in contact with when still in Solingen. He had never told me about that. I did not know yet who I was going to meet in New York.

As we were waiting, I heard my name called over the intercom on the ship. "Mr. Stamm, Mr. Werner Stamm, please come to the Purser's Office."

I thought I did not hear right. But then I heard it again, "Mr. Stamm, please come to the Purser's Office!" I thought, that's me! Did I forget to pay something, a bill?

I found my way to the office. A gentleman there told me, "A Miss Rothchild is waiting for you on the pier." I did not understand. Who?

CHAPTER FIFTY-ONE

MISS ROTHCHILD

I walked back down to the main deck. Cousin Heinz was gone. I walked off the ship and into a large crowd of people milling about.

Miss Rothchild? I had heard of the name Rothchild. A family of millionaires, from Paris, France. And a Miss Rothchild was waiting for me here, in New York, on the pier? Must be a miracle! What does she look like? In my mind, I began to picture a beautiful tall young lady in a mink coat looking for me. How did the Rothchild millionaires know I was arriving in New York? I have arrived in the land of miracles!

As I was standing there craning my neck, I noticed an older short lady in a shabby heavy coat and a floppy hat, carrying some bags. She kept moving closer to me, looking around, and finally stopped, looking at me. I felt rather annoyed, hoping she would go away.

"You Mr. Stamm?" she asked me. "Werner Stamm?"

I looked down at her. "Yes," I said, greatly annoyed. "I am Werner Stamm."

"I am Ms. Rothchild from Traveler's Aid. Welcome to New York! I am going to take you to the train station and to your train to San Francisco."

I had very mixed feelings about her but was grateful that she was there to help me. Then I heard someone calling out my name.

"Werner!" I looked up, and there was Lilo, standing there in all her beauty, my aunt Hetty's best friend, from Solingen. I could not believe it. Lilo had immigrated to the United States two years prior, and she had come to welcome me. We hugged and talked excitedly.

Ms. Rothschild did not seem too pleased. "We have to go, Mr. Stamm!" I found my baggage.

Lilo asked, "May I come along?"

"Sure," I said. "I am so happy to see you!"

Miss Rothchild looked annoyed. We left the harbor and started walking, carrying my baggage. Miss Rothchild was leading the way. She was holding a large paper shopping bag, which she said contained food for me, enough for the three-day trip to San Francisco.

A light rain had started. Our first stop was a Christian church in downtown New York. The church is apparently a well-known New York landmark, buried among huge skyscrapers towering over it. Since I was not a church goer, it did not make much of an impression on me.

It was getting close to lunch time. "I would like to take both of you to a nice restaurant for lunch," Lilo suggested.

Ms. Rothchild shook her head. "No, thank you. We are going to a cafeteria for lunch."

I had no idea what a cafeteria was. We arrived at a place which almost looked like a train station. Inside, and in a straight line, were several machines for dispensing various types of food and drinks. Ms. Rothschild knew what to do. She pushed some buttons, and out came sandwiches wrapped in paper, and cups with soft drinks.

Lilo said to me, "I am very sorry, Werner, but Ms. Rothschild does not want me to be here. I think I should leave." I felt very badly, and sorry to see Lilo leave. We said goodbye. Miss Rothchild and I both had a sandwich.

We then started walking towards Grand Central Station. The rain was getting stronger, and we were getting wet. We reached the station. Ms. Rothchild had tickets and instructions for me. I was taking the train to Chicago. There, I would have a layover of several hours, and then take the California Zephyr train to Oakland, California, across the bay from San Francisco, where I would be met by the Graebe family.

We reached the station and found my train sitting there. Miss Rothchild said, "I will leave you here. Have a good trip." She gave me the large paper bag full of food. I thanked her for helping me and said goodbye.

I never saw Lilo again.

CHAPTER FIFTY-TWO

GOING WEST

The seats on the train were numbered and assigned. I found my seat. I took off my wet winter coat, put my suitcase up on the rack above my head, placed my folded coat on top of it, and my hat on top of the coat. The wet paper bag with the food I kept next to my seat. It was about an hour before the train left. Everything had worked out well so far. I realized that I could not have managed without Ms. Rothchild, and I was extremely grateful to her. But her personality had rubbed me the wrong way. Meeting up with Lilo was such a wonderful surprise, but she had spoiled it for us.

People kept boarding the train. A woman walked up to where I was sitting, checked the seat numbers, and decided that she was sitting across from me. Two porters were with her, carrying several large suitcases. She directed the men to place the suitcases up on the racks around where I was sitting. I did not pay much attention to her or the activity she created.

Finally, the train left the station. I was sitting by the window looking out. We were rolling through New York, forever it seemed. I was shocked to see the neighborhoods the train was traversing. Brick houses without stucco, in various stages of decay, dilapidated. Structures partially collapsed, people walking around in the debris and decay. Was this America, was this the New York I had heard so much about? I was shocked. Gradually we got to what looked like the outskirts of the city, with nice houses surrounded by lawns and scattered trees, and open green areas, with cars moving along on nice roads.

CHAPTER FIFTY-THREE

CHICAGO

We traveled all night. By morning we were traversing rural landscapes with scattered small towns, and occasional stops. Slowly, towns appeared more frequently and were increasing in size. Shortly before noon we slowed down, entering what appeared to be a large city.

"Chicago," people were saying. We finally pulled into a large railroad station and stopped. I waited to let other passengers get off first. Two porters appeared again to help the lady across from me. They pulled down her suitcases, gathered the bags she pointed out to them, and then they all disappeared. I got up after the air had cleared, to get my things together.

I reached up for my hat that I had placed on top of my coat. I could not locate it. After fishing around for it several times unsuccessfully, I climbed up on my seat to look. There was my hat, on top of my coat, just where I had put it, but it was as flat as a pancake. One of the lady's suitcases had apparently been placed on it. I tried to get it back into shape by boxing it out from the inside, but it kept collapsing on me. I pulled down my heavy coat, still soaking wet. I had no choice but to put on my coat, and to put the flat remnant of my hat on my head, before getting down my suitcase and briefcase. I then picked up the paper bag with the food and carried everything outside, setting it down on the concrete pier.

I looked around. People were rushing by on both sides. I pulled out my train tickets. The ticket for my next train was to Oakland, California, on a train called the California Zephyr. Somebody helped me locate the correct pier for the train. I carried all my things there. My train had not yet arrived. I had over three hours until departure. I noticed that other passengers were stashing their suitcases and bags in large lockers at one end of the pier.

I carried my things there also and found an empty locker. Everything fitted inside. I looked around. What should I do for the next three hours? I decided to take a walk into town to see what Chicago looked like.

Once outside the station, I picked one of the streets leading away to what I assumed was downtown Chicago. I decided, that in order not to get lost, I had to stay on that road going and coming back.

I walked for a long time. There was nothing interesting to see. Two- or three-story apartment houses, close together. One thing was changing, though. Gradually I noticed fewer white people, and more colored people on the sidewalks. I finally saw only colored people around me. I came upon three colored children, playing on the sidewalk. I stopped. I had never seen a colored child before. I wanted to take a picture to send home to Solingen.

I got out my camera and took a picture. The children paid no attention to me. Then I heard steps behind me. I looked back. Two colored men were approaching from behind. They were looking at me. I had a sudden feeling in the back of my neck that I should not be there.

I started walking forward past the children. The two men were following behind me and getting closer, I felt. I started walking faster to put more distance between them and me. They started to walk faster also, slowly getting closer. I was beginning to feel very uncomfortable, when I spotted a bar on the corner of a block. I was hoping it was open. I reached the door and pushed. It opened!

I stepped inside and took a deep breath. The two men did not follow me into the bar. I walked over to the bar counter and sat down. "What would you like?" the white bartender said to me.

I looked up. Above me was a sign with a glass of beer and the word Schlitz. That's a German word! I felt terribly relieved.

"One Schlitz, please," I said.

I was served a glass of beer from the tap. The bartender gave me some strange looks, I felt, especially when he was eyeing my collapsed hat, but he said nothing.

I took my time drinking the beer. I paid and walked over to the door. I opened it slightly and carefully, looking in both directions. The two colored men were not in sight. The street seemed empty. I stepped outside and started walking in the direction of the railroad station, as fast as I could. I took a deep breath of relief when I reached the station. I felt safe now.

I found the pier for my train. The train was sitting there. The California Zephyr! It was beautiful. The outside skin of each car was of ribbed stainless steel. And on top of most cars were rows of windows, looking like pilot windows on a fighter plane.

I found my car and my reserved seat. I had a window seat, two seats were facing me, with a small table between. I felt relieved. I had to get the baggage now.

I got everything out of my locker and carried my bags over to the train. As I was getting close to the door of my car, I suddenly noticed the large paper bag with my food was very light. I looked down and saw my food dropping and rolling all over the concrete pier around me. The wet paper bottom of the shopping bag from Miss Rothschild had disintegrated.

What to do? I squatted down to gather the wrapped and canned foods into one pile, sitting and scooting around on the pier. I noticed other passengers skirting around me, giving me disgusting looks. I had to get organized. I carried my suitcase and briefcase inside the train first. The groceries came last. I had three arms full. I deposited them on the wet remnants of the shopping bag, on the empty seat next to me.

Finally, the train started to move and pull out of the station. I could not believe it. It moved totally silently and so softly, like it was floating. I was thinking of the German trains, where each section of rail announced itself with a loud "clang, clang" below. Two more days until San Francisco!

When mealtime came, the passengers got up to go to the dining car. I had no money for that. So, I got out Ms. Rothschild's food and made sandwiches on my little table. It worked out beautifully. We were crossing large, farmed fields with occasional farmhouses, and some forests, hour after hour, until night broke.

CHAPTER FIFTY-FOUR

VISIT TO DENVER

I was looking forward to finally meeting my pen pal Virginia "Ginny" Schoonover in Denver. We had been corresponding for several years, and we felt like friends, although we had never met. Ginny had sent me food packages to Germany when times were hard there, and she also sent me sheet music for piano, such as "In the Mood," and "Chattanooga Choo Choo," which I had used in our dance band in Solingen.

When I wrote to her that I was immigrating to the U.S, the whole family was delighted and was anxious to meet me. I had told them about my travel plans in advance. They insisted that I stop in Denver on my way west, to meet them.

The Schoonovers found out about my delayed arrival in New York and the changed train schedule. When I finally arrived in Denver, the entire family was at the station, waiting for me, giving me a wonderful welcome. The train was scheduled to stop there for several hours before continuing to Oakland/San Francisco in California.

The Schoonover family told me that I was going to stay with them for two days before continuing to California. I did not know what to say. They called my sponsors, the Graebe family in San Francisco, telling them about my delay, and they arranged the change in my train ticket.

I got my things off the train, and we all got into the family car. A beautiful car. It was a Packard. We arrived at their house, located in a middle to upper class neighborhood on a tree-lined street, with lawns in front. All single-family homes, mainly British Tudor style.

Beautiful, I thought. There was nothing like that in Solingen. And everybody seemed to have a car. My parents and I had just had one bicycle, the company bicycle.

The Schoonover family made me feel really special. Ginny's dad had died several years before. He had been a doctor and had practiced general medicine. Now there was Ginnie's mother, Mrs. Schoonover, and Ginnie's brother Jack. Ginny was a very nice-looking brunette. Her voice sounded a little rough. She was a chain smoker. Ginny had gotten engaged a year before I arrived. I met her fiancé, a very nice soft-spoken guy, also by the name of Jack.

I was given a bedroom upstairs. Somehow the two days with the family seemed to fly by rapidly. On the second evening we all went to see a movie, Snow White and the Seven Dwarfs, a Disney film which had just been released. The movie theater alone was spectacular in its decorations and comfortable upholstered seats. Our Solingen movie theater was a converted gymnasium, with hard chairs set up in rows.

We talked about many things, including my plans for the future. I told them that I wanted to study medicine, to become a doctor. (I talked to Ginny's brother Jack many years later, when attending a medical conference in Denver. He told me that he and the family knew that the study of medicine was very difficult, and they did not believe that I could succeed, considering all the problems I was facing.)

After two days, my time with the Schoonover family was up. They took me back to the train station and we said goodbye. I felt that I had been with good, true friends. The California Zephyr arrived and took me away. Goodbye, my Colorado friends! California, here I come!

CHAPTER FIFTY-FIVE

CALIFORNIA, I HAVE ARRIVED!

After we left Denver, the train started to climb. We were entering the region of the Rocky Mountains. The scenery became spectacular, snow-covered mountain peaks alternating with green meadows in the valleys.

I followed the other passengers up a small staircase in the cars into the Vista Domes, for the most beautiful views imaginable. Up there your head and shoulders were above the level of the roof of the train cars, giving you a spectacular 360-degree view of the entire area. In the higher elevations of the mountains, I could see cars from our train in two or three different tunnels at the same time, slowly winding our way west. I was hoping it would never end. But slowly the train descended in many twists and turns to enter a sunny large hilly landscape below.

We entered a small station in a small town. A tall palm tree stood next to the tracks. It was the first palm tree I had ever seen in my life. I have never forgotten it. We were in California, and now heading towards Oakland and San Francisco.

A couple was seated across from me. We introduced ourselves to each other. Dr. and Mrs. Johnson from Alameda, California. Dr. Johnson was in the practice of general medicine. When I told them I was coming to California to study medicine, they became very interested in my story. We exchanged addresses and promised to stay in contact with each other. Since Alameda was not far from San

Francisco, we might even visit one another, they suggested. I happily agreed.

Evening was approaching, and daylight was slowly receding. An announcement came over the intercom. We were approaching Oakland, California, our final destination. The train started to slow down and began to rattle through some switches. It finally stopped. I felt very nervous. I had arrived at my destination. What was awaiting me there?

Passengers were getting up, shouting, getting their baggage down from the racks, and rushing towards the doors. I waited until the rush subsided, got my belongings together and headed for the door. I got outside and looked around. And there they were, walking towards me, waving. My Solingen friends, Fred Graebe and his parents greeted me.

After a lot of hugging and happy shouting, Fred told me that we were taking the ferry boat across San Francisco Bay to San Francisco, where they lived. We walked to the nearby boat pier and got on the ferry. Shortly thereafter the boat left the pier, and we were heading into the bay.

What a sight in front of me! Dusk had set in, and the sky had turned a purple red, reflecting its colors in the water. We were approaching a huge bridge, the Bay Bridge, its structure lit up by thousands of lights. In the distance, I saw the outlines of very tall buildings with millions of lights, it seemed. San Francisco! In the far distance to the right, more huge arches of lights, in a wondrous display. The Golden Gate Bridge, I was told. I felt overwhelmed. This was going to be my new home. I could not speak any more. I felt so lucky, so fortunate, so grateful.

CHAPTER FIFTY-SIX

MY MOTHER'S STORIES

When reading these lines and reflecting over them, I realize that the true hero or heroine in this story is my mother, Mrs. Anna Stamm. She was a woman of rare qualities. Of courage, of determination, of love, of loyalty, with a great sense of humor and love of life, all thrown into one.

She had many friends, generally of her own age. As she got older and moved into her eighties and then nineties, most of her friends had passed away, and she adopted a new circle of people a generation younger, namely my friends.

I have often wondered what gave her the courage and determination she displayed, especially during the years of World War II, and the difficult post war years. I realize that her character was probably shaped by her experiences as a teenage girl during the years of World War I, which lasted from 1914 to 1918. Many of the stories she told relate back to that period.

1917 was a year when much of the German city population was starving. My mother was 13 at that time. Together with other children from the cities, she was shipped by train to the provinces of rural eastern Germany, where the children would live with farmers' families.

These are some of the stories she told.

The train full of children from West Germany slowly chugged along through the rural landscape of Eastern Germany. Each child wore around their neck a tag with the name of the adopting farmer's family and the name of the village. The train would stop at each small town or village, and the local farmers would be standing there, holding a sign bearing the name of the child they were adopting. At one stop, a single farmer stood there holding up the name of my mother's 10-year-old brother Willi. Mother did not like the looks of that man. She quickly tore the tag from her brother's neck and told him to stay in his seat and be quiet. No child got off, and the train moved on. Finally, my mother's name came up. She got off the train with Willi. Nobody wanted Willi. But Mother insisted that her brother stay with her. She won. Both she and her brother were adopted by the same family. Both lived with the farmer and his family until World War I ended in 1918. Mother used to like to tell stories of their time on the farm.

The farm kitchen was always full of black flies. They used to sit on the ceiling, especially above the kitchen stove. When the farmer's wife made soup, she used a large kettle. When the lid was removed to stir the soup, the hot steam rose to the ceiling, and dozens of flies would drop down and into the soup. Mother thought that nobody could eat that soup. But the farmers would calmly move the dead flies to the rim of the plate and enjoy the soup.

Little brother Willi loved to play in the hay barn. Some of the chickens would build nests in the hay and lay their eggs there. Often Willi would take one of the eggs, crack open the shell and suck out the contents. One day, as he was sucking out an egg, he ended up with a chick embryo in his throat. He never sucked out an egg again.

Mother was put in charge of guarding the newly born chicks outside, in a small, fenced area. One day, with the little chicks outside, Mother was reading a book. She noticed too late that it had started to rain. The chicks got soaking wet, which could mean their death. She quickly scooped up the chicks into her apron, ran into the house, and put them under the kitchen stove to dry out. The heat killed all the chicks.

Mother was to herd the cows. She had to keep them moving and feeding on the grass in the meadow, so that they would produce enough milk and gain weight. One day Mother found a book she liked. She sat on the grassy meadow and started reading. She did not notice that the cows had followed her example. All were lying down in the meadow instead of foraging. Mother got a beating from the farmer.

Acknowledgements

The writing of this book would not have been possible without the encouragement, guidance and assistance of my two sons, Richard Stamm and Allan Stamm.

I must especially thank my son Allan for his patience and guidance in helping me with the technical aspect of this composition, a task which I had never undertaken before.

My friend the jazz pianist Glen Rose and my neighbor Amber McClain Shaw also have donated much time and effort toward this work and deserve special recognition.

ABOUT THE AUTHOR

Dr. Werner Stamm was born in Solingen, Germany, in 1931, son of a knifemaker. As a child, he experienced first-hand the trials of World War II, and the almost equally difficult first few post war years. He immigrated to the United States at age 20, in 1952. He initially lived with his sponsors, the Graebe family, in San Francisco, California.

He worked several jobs to pay off his debts. He enrolled at San Francisco City College and later at the University of California, Berkeley. He was accepted at the University of California San Francisco School of Medicine in 1954. He received his MD degree in 1958 and took a one-year rotating internship at San Joaquin General Hospital in Stockton, California, followed by a four-year residency in clinical and anatomic pathology at O'Connor Hospital in San Jose, California.

Dr. Stamm was Board Certified in Anatomic and Clinical Pathology in 1963, and entered the private practice of Pathology in Santa Cruz, California in 1964, as a member of APMG (Associated Pathology Medical Group). In that capacity, he worked in Hospital Practice as well as in Medicolegal Practice for the Coroner's Office of Santa Cruz County.

He retired from work at age 65 but was invited to rejoin his medical group two years later. He worked for 20 more years in private pathology practice, retiring at age 87.